MW00510597

A PASSION FOR STEWARDSHIP

THE LEGACY OF A GENERATION

Richard A. Johanson

First Edition

An
Auberry Press
Publication

Johanson, Richard A.

A Passion for Stewardship: The Legacy of a Generation/Richard A. Johanson – 1st Edition

ISBN: 978-0-9778784-1-3

1. Biography 2. Autobiography 3. WWII 4. The Great Depression

Inquiries:

Auberry Press
2037 West Bullard Avenue #427
Fresno, California 93711
info@auberrypress.com

Cover Design: Allison B. Boogaert

Published by:

Auberry Press
www.auberrypress.com

DEDICATION

To My Mom and Dad

Carrie and Hilmer Johanson

To My Wife

Althea

To Our Children

Larry and his wife Patti
Gale and her husband Jason Gomes

To Our Grandchildren

Amanda and Yvonne Johanson
Jody Gomes

INTRODUCTION

We live in rapidly changing, rootless times with a backdrop of anxiety and even dread about the future. Our leaders seem ill equipped to govern, much less inspire us to a higher purpose. While at one time I looked to leaders who could convince me that they would keep me safe and make everything right, I have learned that no such people exist, if they ever really did. No one really knows what will happen next or if a certain course of action will work. However, in spite of not knowing, some people have the courage and humility to take the reins anyway, trusting that together and with the help of internal guidance, they will work together with us to find our way.

I asked Dick Johanson to write his memoirs for many reasons. He is a fine writer with a rich repertoire of insightful and wise sayings. He led the Fresno Business Council, a CEO business group, during our challenging early years when the notion of stewardship was foreign and antithetical to some who believed leadership is about power, not service. Finally, as a Baby Boomer, I thought it critical that one of the thoughtful members of The Greatest Generation could help us understand the life experiences and beliefs that shaped them. In doing so, it is hoped that more people will be inspired to make integrity, humility and service the touchstones of their lives.

After reading the manuscript, I wept. I was so deeply moved by his story. I felt both sadness and fear as I wondered whether or not my generation and those to come are able and willing to take the torch that is being passed to us. My hope is that Dick's story and his honor and his dignity find their way into the hearts of the Baby Boomers and those coming up behind them. My further hope would be that the legacy of his generation will ignite a passion for service and community that The Greatest Generation demonstrated for decades.

We did have one disagreement. In an early version, Dick criticized those in my generation that tried to bring down institutions, got lost in drugs and promiscuity and became self-indulgent. I suggested that the shadow of his generation gave us Viet Nam and Watergate and some people simply became cynical and dropped out. Others got caught up in materialism while some continued to work for the American Dream of liberty and justice for all. Every generation has its light and its shadows. Hopefully, we can learn to build upon the strengths of each generation and move the torch along toward a world where poverty, war and discrimination are present only in history books and peace, justice, and prosperity exist across the global community.

Deborah J. Nankivell

TABLE OF CONTENTS

CHAPTER III – 1946 TO 1971

CHAPTER IV – BIRTHING A BUSINESS

CHAPTER I - 1925 TO 1942

THE JOURNEY BEGINS

Some years ago former NBC News Anchor Tom Brokaw wrote a book entitled "The Greatest Generation." As a member of that generation I have reflected often on the circumstances that caused him to describe my generation as he did. Those of us who are part of it lived through the stock market crash of 1929. We lived through the Great Depression. We survived the horrors of World War II. We were advocates for democracy during détente of the Cold War and the social agonies of the Viet Nam era. Currently, we are sharing the dangers and tensions of secular terrorism. Through all of this, my generation has struggled passionately to bring about a world of peace with opportunity for a life free from hunger and strife.

After extensive soul searching and at the urging of someone to whom I have long turned for counsel, this is my attempt to adapt Mr. Brokaw's overview of "The Greatest Generation" into a single person's perspective. It is my purpose in this narrative to describe events in my life that were important to me and, hopefully, will be of interest to the reader.

A companion hope is that those of succeeding generations will come to understand and appreciate the hopes and dreams that the members of my generation still possess. It is my profound prayer that those who became discouraged with the affairs of this nation in the '60s and '70s will find a way to once again become encouraged as we move forward into a new century. It is my hope that all may take from this chronicle an assurance that we shall never reach our constitutionally-defined destiny without the enlightened participation of those stewards who are destined to lead us.

I am thankful also for all of those public and private figures who had a positive influence upon my long life. I am hopeful that these recordings contain within them important elements helping to define the cultural and moral values for which my generation is receiving credit. How I perceived these events and why they remain important to me is unquestionably due in part to those characteristics imbedded in me by my parents and family as well as so many other dear friends.

Here then is the story of a life of eighty plus years written in a spirit of love and sharing with all who may peruse it. This story will, of necessity, be open ended because the Greatest Generation, while rapidly dwindling in numbers, still retains its long held fervor for achieving a permanent solution to the many cultural, social, and economic problems existing throughout our nation and our world. This story is primarily focused in the heart of the state of California. While it is overtly a story about my family and me, it is also the story of many who came to California to find a new beginning based on deep-seated values that were formed over many generations.

As we start this journey it will be helpful to reconstruct a basic outline of my life from my earliest years through high school. As the narrative continues, it is my intention that the reader will grasp how many of these childhood experiences became the foundation for decisions and events that occurred later in my life. It is how these events and decisions unfolded and were handled that formed the foundation for the Greatest Generation description proposed by Mr. Brokaw and others.

Let us begin by discussing a bit about my heritage. In learning the roots of my mom and my dad, you will discover a reason or two for my admiration for both of them. You may also get an insight as to why it was so important for me to conduct my life in such a manner as to be worthy of their unconditional love and respect.

My father immigrated to the United States from Sweden at the age of seven along with his parents and four brothers. Ultimately he would be one of twelve children, ten of whom lived to adulthood. They settled on a farm southwest of Fresno near the small unincorporated town of Monmouth. Upon arrival in this country, my father immediately enrolled in the first grade of the Monmouth grammar school. He could speak only a minimal amount of English. In this day of educational issues regarding second languages it is interesting to remember him recalling how his mother and father would try to speak only English rather than Swedish in front of their children after arrival in this country. Their rationale was that "this was America and English was the language of the land." An amusing cultural aside is that there were few Swedes and lots of Danes in the area. Grounded in a deep desire to become more socially acceptable, some of my uncles even changed the spelling of their last name from Johanson to Johansen.

Like so many others of his time, my dad was only able to complete an elementary school formal education. He was almost sixteen when he graduated from grammar school. He immediately went to work at the newly constructed Sun-Maid Raisin Growers processing and storage facility in Monmouth. He often recalled that, during his younger years, his justification for not continuing his formal education was built around the fact that he could earn two dollars and fifty cents a day working at the raisin plant.

In 1914 World War I engulfed central Europe. England, France and the United States confronted Kaiser Wilhelm and the German military forces. In 1918 my dad was drafted and ordered to report for induction into the United States Army. Two of my uncles had already enlisted in the armed forces - one in the Army and the other in the Marine Corps. Dad told us that he was actually at the train station in Fresno, ready to depart for duty, when word was received that the four year war had ended. He returned home without being officially sworn into military service. Shortly after he returned home, he obtained employment with the Standard Oil Company of California. His new job consisted of driving a truck delivering gasoline and oil to the many farms and businesses within his assigned territory. His first job location was the distribution plant in Kingsburg, located twenty miles south of Fresno.

My mother was born in Chicago, Illinois, to parents who immigrated to this country from the northeastern part of Germany, which became Poland at the conclusion of World War I. She was raised in the inner city and said many times that she never saw the open countryside nor her first live cow until she was sixteen years of age. She also had an education that basically ended at eighth grade and was self-educated beyond that formal level. When her father died at a young age, she moved with her mother, brothers, and sisters to Portland, Oregon. Some time later she followed one of her sisters to Kingsburg to work as a waitress in her sister's restaurant located on Draper Street, the main street in town. It was in that restaurant that my father and mother met.

A courtship ensued, followed by a proposal of marriage from my dad, which my mother happily accepted subject to a faith-based caveat. My mother was a devout Catholic while my father belonged to the Lutheran church, as did most folks of Scandinavian ancestry. While the two churches have some similarities, my father did consent to the Catholic dogma that any children resulting from the marriage would be reared in the Catholic faith. Both of their fathers had passed away while they were still teenagers so they decided to be married in the presence of my maternal grandmother and her family in Oregon. The wedding took place in the small town of St. Helens, downstream about forty miles along the Columbia River from the emerging metropolis of Portland. My father and his best man made the trek in three days from Kingsburg to Portland via a Model T Ford. Mom and dad were married on June 19, 1923.

A FAMILY IS FORMED

Carrie and Hilmer Johanson established their first home in Fresno. It was a rental located on Belmont Avenue directly across from Roeding Park. The exact location is now part of the right of way along California State Highway 99 freeway. In addition to his daytime job driving a gasoline delivery truck on a route centered around Fresno, my father continued his education by taking classes at Fresno Technical High School in the evening. This site later became Fresno Junior College, the first junior college in the State of California. It is presently the site of the Cesar Chavez Adult School operated by the Fresno Unified School District.

Two and a half years later in December 1925, I was born at the Barnett Sanitarium, now the site of the Community Medical Centers Hospital complex in downtown Fresno. While my mother was pregnant with me, she contacted malaria and lost much of her hearing capability. To her credit she became an accomplished lip reader since hearing aids were not readily available nor, in our case, affordable. I continue to believe that this personal handicap, combined with her faith and compassion for others, contributed to her desire to understand and serve those in need throughout her long life.

Shortly after I arrived on the scene my father was transferred north to the hamlet of Gregg in Madera County, which no longer exists. I retain my earliest memories from the time that we lived in Gregg. The first of these was the love that my mom and dad had for each other and for those about them. Both of my grandfathers passed away long before I was born and I never had the opportunity to know either of them. However, I did get to know my grandmothers. My mom's mother lived in Oregon so I only saw her once or twice. She died while I was just beginning elementary school. My dad's mother still resided on the family farm in Monmouth and lived until I was in the seventh grade. Grandma Johanson spoke very broken English and was fun to be around. The best pronunciation she could do with my given name sounded like "Aitsa".

Our home in Gregg was a combination residence, store, and post office. While my father was delivering gasoline to the surrounding area, my mother kept the household and operated the little store and post office. Each day she would take the small sack of outgoing mail and affix the mail sack to a devise that suspended it alongside the railroad track. As the passenger train sped by, a worker in the baggage car would throw off the incoming mail and scoop away the outgoing mail. While I was much too small to know how much income the store and post office generated, the revenue could not have been very great. It is worth noting that Gregg was a fairly remote location among cotton and grain fields. There was no rural mail delivery system so all who resided in that semi-remote post office service area were compelled to come to the post office to send and receive their mail and, hopefully, buy staples for daily use and planning. In 1928 and 1929 journeying to Madera or Fresno for supplies consumed most of a day. As vehicles and roads improved and travel times were shortened, this little oasis, like so many others throughout the area, gradually lessened in economic significance. Today it has totally disappeared.

It was here that something happened that was the course of conversational delight to my mom and dad for many years. I developed a chronic sore throat and the doctor decided I needed to have my tonsils removed. One Saturday morning my folks took me to Madera to have the surgery done. I can still recall the smell of the ether in the doctor's office. I can also remember the bumpy car ride home that same afternoon. The next day was Sunday and my mother went to church only after telling my dad that he was to make sure that I remained in the house and preferably in bed. It was not long after she left that I began to feel much better. My dad offered me some cookies and milk. By the time my mother returned from church I was outside riding my tricycle. Needless to say there was some internal family consternation because my grandmother made the long trip from Monmouth to Gregg to visit her little grandson who had just undergone a "serious" operation! I remember greeting her from my little red tricycle. I was three and a half years old.

Another snapshot from that era had to do with our neighbors who lived across a field from us. We had electricity in our home. They did not. I retain vivid memories of visiting them and watching them light kerosene lamps as darkness arrived. The jumping shadows on the walls from the flickering light in the dimly lit rooms created visions of frightening dragons in my young mind.

It was in Gregg that my brother Paul was born. It was not long after Paul arrived that my father was transferred once again. This time we moved to the town of Kerman about fifteen miles west of Fresno. After living amid the cotton and grain fields of Madera County, living in Kerman with a population of 700 or 800 was like living in a metropolis. In September 1931, at the age of five, my mom took me to the Kerman elementary school where I enrolled in the first grade. I loved school. I also learned how to be "momma's helper." It was a walk of five or six blocks from the school to our house. Every afternoon on my way home from school I would stop at the grocery store and pick up a quart of milk. No charge cards in those days. The clerk would handwrite the details of the purchase on a sales tag and place it in the cash register. Periodically my mom or dad would pay the accumulated charges for the milk as well as for any groceries they had purchased. Three months after school started, my second brother Howard, was born at home. My most vivid memory of his arrival is how wrinkly he looked the first time I saw him!

During the following summer my father received a promotion to Head Area Salesman at San Joaquin and hence we moved once again. Our new home was located in the semi-remoteness of the San Joaquin Valley's emerging "West Side." Pop still drove a delivery truck but he was now in charge of one other employee as well as having responsibility for the company's storage and delivery facility. We remained there six years during which time I completed elementary school.

San Joaquin's newly constructed elementary school consisted of four classrooms. Each teacher taught two grades. The principal taught grades seven and eight. His wife taught grades one and two. We were a happy bunch of kids. For the first two or three years that we lived in town we walked the half-dozen blocks to and from school.

An amusing moment occurred while walking home after my first day of school in the second grade. Like a dutiful son trying to help his mom, I stopped at the grocery store, took a bottle of milk and proceeded to walk out of the store with it. Fortunately, the storekeeper already knew my dad and had no problem figuring out who I was and who was going to pay the bill. My father often joked that neither he, nor anyone else, ever had trouble finding his fair-haired Swedish kids among all the black-haired Italians and Portuguese townspeople.

Later my folks moved further out into the country. They rented a small house located across an alfalfa field from the residence and dairy farm owned by good friends. It was not long before my brothers and I learned to clean out the barn, herd the cows, feed them hay, and ride horses. Nearby was the residence of the school principal and his wife. They volunteered to let my brothers and me ride to and from school with them in their car so we only occasionally rode the official school bus. What a great life for three young boys. What a pleasure it is to reflect upon these rich memories.

While I was in the third grade my parents were asked, prior to Christmas vacation, if they would allow the school to promote me to the fourth grade for the rest of the school year. They agreed. The following fall I entered the fifth grade. Because I had entered first grade while I was still five years old, I was now two years younger than my classmates. My new class group consisted of four girls and three boys. We remained together all through the rest of our grammar school years.

An amusing sidebar to these promotions is that because of my youth and small size, I picked up the nickname of "quarter." The principal said I was too small to be called "half pint!" I recall that as he was preparing his enrollment book for the eighth grade, he had to ask me for my real first name. After my six classmates and I sat onstage and proudly received our eighth grade graduation certificates and after I had enrolled to attend high school in the neighboring town of Tranquility, my father received word that he was being transferred once again.

It was during the grammar school years of our lives that my brothers and I subconsciously became indoctrinated with the meaning of family values. Grandma Johanson still lived in the same home she occupied when she came to this country from Sweden many years ago.

There is no childhood memory stronger than going to Gramma Jo's on Sunday afternoon. Dinner was usually served in her large dining room at about 2 p.m. The meal invariably consisted of crisply fried chicken, frothy mashed potatoes, bowls of creamy gravy, homemade bread, freshly churned butter and a garden vegetable or two. Dessert was generous scoops of super rich hand-cranked homemade ice cream from milk provided by Gramma's family cow. Late afternoon was spent on the front lawn recovering from Gramma's irresistible cooking and sharing joy with aunts, uncles and cousins.

As evening approached, each family member would end the day giving Gramma a big hug and head for home. For us it was an hour's ride back to San Joaquin. Happiness lies in the reflections of simple things. My mind is still rich with the simple memories of my dad's wonderful family enjoying hours together.

Midsummer 1938 saw us packing our belongings and relocating to the lovely Swedish heritage town of Kingsburg where my mother and father had met twenty-five years earlier. It was a wonderful homecoming for both of them. That fall I entered Kingsburg High School as a wide-eyed twelve-year-old undersized freshman weighing 79 pounds. My two brothers entered the local grammar schools. While it was difficult to leave our many friends in San Joaquin, it was only a short time until we were immersed in the excitement of our new schools and newly made friends. To this day I refer to Kingsburg as my hometown.

Throughout the next three years, a pattern evolved that may have set the tone for much of my life that was to follow. Working and playing with others in various school and community organizations became a way of life. School plays, intramural sports (I was never big enough to play on a varsity team), school clubs, music, Boy Scouts, and church activities, all became part of a happy, meaningful, and busy lifestyle. I still found time to earn some spending money mowing lawns, picking grapes, and other miscellaneous jobs such as working as a "milk hop" delivering milk to homes and stores while hanging onto the side of a pickup truck.

During my junior year, my father decided to leave the Standard Oil Company for whom he had worked for so many years and became an appliance store manager for an up and coming new firm. With his many contacts throughout the central valley, he became quite successful. In the summer of 1941 he accepted an offer to become manager of an appliance store in the San Francisco Bay Area town of Lafayette. So, rather than graduating from Kingsburg High School, I transferred to Concord High School for my senior year. I graduated in the spring of 1942. During that school year, during which time we had moved from Lafayette to the nearby small hamlet of Alamo, my third brother Walter was born.

THE GREAT DEPRESSION

It's time to take careful look back at the unprecedented economic hardship suffered within this country between the collapse of the stock market in October 1929, and the beginning of World War II. Upon the virtual disintegration of the nation's economic base, this country entered a depression unlike any endured before or since. Paper fortunes disappeared like hail falling upon warm pavement. Families suffered financial ruin overnight. Booming businesses suddenly became bankrupt. Banks barricaded their doors. Factories were shut down. Thousands upon thousands of working people were suddenly unemployed with little or no chance of finding replacement jobs anywhere. Highly skilled professionals were reduced to working in menial jobs. It was not unusual to see persons with advanced university degrees working as clerks in grocery stores or as attendants in gasoline stations. There was no governmental program in place for any form of financial assistance to those in need. Despair prevailed throughout nearly every level of American society.

In our family's case, because my father's employer produced and delivered necessary oil and gasoline primarily to rural customers, my father's job was relatively secure. However, his monthly paycheck of sixty-seven dollars did not provide more than the barest necessities for our family. I have no way of knowing whether his numerous job transfers were directly related to the depressed economy,

Interestingly, however, I cannot recall a time when I ever felt that we were poor. The closeness of our family and the inherent love and wisdom of my mom and pop gave us a wealth that extended well beyond dollars and cents. In the recent years of my life I have thought often of this paradox. Poorness has become the antithesis of materialism. On all sides we are being assaulted with pressures that our stature in life is measured by our physical possessions. As kids, the joy in our lives came from an appreciation of what we had rather than envy for what we did not have.

In November of 1932 the nation overwhelmingly elected a new president with a new vision. Although physically handicapped, having suffered from polio, Franklin Delano Roosevelt exuded an Ivy League assurance that his policies would lead the nation back to prosperity. Shortly after his election he began an ongoing series of radio "fireside chats." Slowly the populace began to develop confidence in our nation's ability to reinvigorate its economy. His widespread popularity would allow him to become the only president in this nation's history to be elected to a fourth term.

Between the time of his election and the beginning of World War II President Roosevelt and the Congress enacted numerous public assistance programs. All were designed to alleviate the burden of hunger and joblessness facing the nation's multitudes. This innovative legislation was a milestone turnaround from the laissez-faire policy that existed prior to that time. The Civilian Conservation Corps legislation was passed whereby young people could work on our nationally owned lands for nominal wages. The Works Progress Administration was enacted. This program created thousands of jobs by funding badly needed government projects throughout the land. Congress further enacted the Social Security program to provide for an income for wage earners upon reaching retirement age. I vividly remembering my father excitingly describing how, upon reaching the age of sixty-five, he would receive a check for over two hundred dollars per month for the rest of his life.

However, all of these programs did not obscure the fact that the nation remained mired in an economic meltdown. The sobering events during these depression years made a tremendous impact upon those of us who, at school age then, now comprise today's "Older Americans."

A few indelible pictures. Begging became a necessary and acceptable way of life. Today many of our street people have created their own misery through the misuse of drugs and alcohol. In 1934 when someone knocked on your backdoor asking for food, they were there because there was no work to be found and they were hungry. These were, quite often, reputable men and women who were caught up in an economic stagnancy beyond their control. My mother often found little "make work" tasks for these unfortunate people who were dubbed hoboes by some. My mother's purpose was to give them the dignity of feeling that they had worked for their small meal. There was tremendous transience, most noticeably among the men, who left the bigger cities where there was no longer work. These "kings of the road" traveled as uninvited guests on freight trains trying to find employment wherever they could. They were not bad people. They were good people having bad luck. California became a magnet for hope. As a young boy I remember being told that "hoboes" had a way of identifying homes where handouts were likely. Because we lived less than two blocks from the railroad tracks we oftentimes thought ours was somehow "marked."

Those of my generation who were fortunate to be living in a relatively stable environment could not avoid developing a compassion for the unfortunate through these experiences. It was an era of those who could "spare a dime" willingly helping those without a penny. As stated earlier, at the outset there were no governmental assistance programs to which the distressed could turn for assistance. Such programs did not exist or were newly emerging and not yet broad based enough to affect the masses.

To offset the absence of government supported aid programs in the beginning years of the Depression, throughout the land there existed an understated but implicit understanding that those in a position to do so would willingly assist those in need. It was not uncommon to hear a knock on the backdoor and be asked for permission to sleep in the garage or barn or yard. Pictures like these are etched in one's mind for a lifetime. Perhaps somewhere within this experience, the seeds of caring for others less fortunate than ourselves were deeply planted. It is this ethic that became a root structure for the strength of compassion and commitment to volunteerism that exists so deeply within this generation.

On an international basis, it was out of this same sense of responsibility for the less fortunate among the people of the world that the Marshall Plan was created at the conclusion of World War II. Our nation accepted a responsibility for accelerating a return to economic normalcy among those nations who had been both our bitter enemies and our staunch allies during four long years of violent strife.

A WORD ABOUT "OKIES"

On the local scene, in addition to all of those transients who had once held productive jobs and were now without work, we had another wave of unfortunates come among us. The once bountiful middle southern states were suffering an on-going draught that doomed the region to become known as the Dust Bowl. Thousands upon thousands of desperate hard-working farmers from Kansas, Oklahoma, Arkansas, and Texas were forced to abandon their farms. Thousands more whose livelihood depended upon a prosperous agricultural economy were without employment.

Most of these folks had no recourse but to migrate elsewhere. Taking what few possessions they had, they began the long trek toward a new life. Many of them opted for California to find seasonal jobs as field workers. It was a way of subsistence for these unfortunates, commonly but not derisively referred to as "Okies", to work in the fields, orchards, and vineyards harvesting the maturing crops. John Steinbeck captured this poignant piece of history in his epic novel "The Grapes of Wrath". It should be noted that as the years passed by the children of these hardy families grew into adulthood and today comprise a significant part of the Greatest Generation.

In the small semi-isolated agriculturally based community of San Joaquin, to which I referred earlier, the school building that was no longer used when the new school was opened would be reopened for only a few weeks each fall. For this brief period of time the children of the "Okie" migrant cotton pickers (all cotton was picked by hand at that time) could go to school while their parents were working in the surrounding fields. I vividly remember those of us who were permanent residents watching the temporary teachers in the old school inspect the migrant children's hair during lunchtime and recess to remove any fleas or ticks that might be present. There was rarely running water or other indoor facilities in the primitive labor camps where the transients stayed for the short time they were in the area picking cotton.

It is important to understand that semi-poverty also affected permanent residents as well. I shall never forget cutting up pasteboard to insert inside the bottom of our shoes to cover the holes so that the soles of our feet we would not touch the bare ground as we walked to and from school. We did not consider ourselves poor. We had a roof over our heads, running water, and a permanent home. We had the love and security of our parents and each other.

In retrospect, while I was still only of grammar school age, I developed a deep sense of compassion for the education of all children. Each of us is provided parents without preconceived input as to their suitability. Some of us have been extremely lucky in having moms and dads whose prime concern in their lives was to provide better lives for their children. Among those were the dust bowl parents. Some of us had the misfortune to be born into dysfunctional family situations. In both situations, as children we were not the controllers. As we matured into adulthood, however, we assumed the burden of accepting what had been provided to us and worked diligently to build successful lives each in our own way. Ironically, the Great Depression brought out both the best and worst of what was possible.

From this it is fair to deduce that it is up to caring parents, a caring community, and a compassionate government to ensure that all kids are given the opportunity to grow into well-rounded adults. Fundamental to any progress in this effort is ensuring that all children are educated to best of our society's ability to do so. While today many of our schools and many of our children are not at the levels expected of them, I submit that the Greatest Generation folks are passionate about academic achievement. This powerful drive is based upon our memories of the struggles by so many to learn while lacking basic educational facilities, stability, and funding during the Great Depression. There is a great similarity between the displaced domestic migrants of the thirties and the multi-national immigrants of today.

It is unthinkable to leave this segment of our journey without paying special tribute to the generation of hard-working moms and dads who reared the men and women that Mr. Brokaw identifies as members of the "Greatest Generation." Out of despair came hope. Out of hope came opportunity. Out of opportunity came compassion. Out of compassion came dedication. Out of dedication came transformation. These strongly principled men and women knew the tragedy of World War I. They had pioneered the development of our nation, particularly the newly opened western states. They had survived the stock market debacle of 1929 and suffered through the Great Depression that followed. They had faith in our country and its capacity to act as a haven for the oppressed from wherever they would come. They will always remain an inspiration to those of us who followed them. Very obviously, high among these were my mom and dad.

THE DAY OF INFAMY

Everything changed on a Sunday morning in December 1941. For most of us, the Hawaiian Islands were only a tropical fantasy far out in the Pacific Ocean. To others they were a paradise romanticized in black-and-white movies starring a sarong-clad Dorothy Lamoure. Most of us were faintly aware that Pearl Harbor was located on the island of Oahu and home to the Pacific Fleet of the U. S. Navy. It commanded very little if any attention in our schoolbooks or our daily newspapers.

The defining crescendo for those of us who are living the Greatest Generation experience was December 7, 1941. More than any act in our history, in the opinion of most historians, the attack on Pearl Harbor by the Imperial Japanese Fleet unified this nation in a common purpose as never before. We came together with a determination to protect our way of life based upon our constitutional guarantees and reinforced by our national pride.

Our family was at home in Alamo, that infamous Sunday morning, preparing to leave for church when word arrived via radio that Pearl Harbor was being bombed by the Japanese. That afternoon my folks drove us to the movie theater in nearby Walnut Creek. They returned home for a few hours to try to digest the implications of that morning's newscast. An interesting aside is that my younger brother, Howard, still remembers that the movie we saw was "Sergeant York," a hero of World War I, starring Gary Cooper.

The following evening our family all gathered around our radio and listened to President Roosevelt deliver his famous "Day of Infamy" speech to the Congress and the nation. Our country was now in a state of war with Japan in the Pacific and Asia. We were also at war with Germany and Italy in the Atlantic and Europe. Almost over night, this country was redirected from emerging itself from a demoralizing Depression-focused economy into a bustling flurry of wartime-oriented activities. This life or death effort would demand all of our energy to provide the goods and services required to successfully wage a land and sea war across two vast oceans.

With all of the nation's resources now centered on successfully waging a worldwide war, the use of scarce metals to manufacture new domestic products was severely curtailed. Consumer items such as automobiles and appliances made primarily from metal soon became unavailable or extremely scarce. It was not too long before the company employing my dad was forced to shut down because of a lack of inventory. However, unlike the depths of the Great Depression when jobs became non-existent, war-related jobs were readily available. My father immediately went to work for a shipbuilding company in Albany, on the eastern shore of San Francisco Bay.

A BRIEF TASTE OF HIGHER EDUCATION

While all of these world-changing events were transpiring, I graduated from Concord High School in the spring of 1942. Some months prior to graduation, a school counselor brought to my attention that my grade point average entitled me to apply for admission to the University of California. It was a happy experience to share this exciting news with my mom and dad. By enrolling at the university I would become the first member of our extended family to attend any accredited college level institution.

In September 1942, I walked onto the campus of the University of California in Berkeley as a sixteen-year-old freshman. I had no clear idea of what career path I wished to pursue. Therefore, I declared my major to be my favorite subject, which was history. A requirement of all University male students was enrollment in the on-campus Reserve Officer Training Corps program. It was my introduction to a military environment. All able young men were subject to be drafted into the military upon reaching the age of eighteen. Almost all draftees were inducted into the Army. I never made inquiry as to whether undergoing R.O.T.C training at the university would have deferred my service. With a sense of overwhelming pride, I decided that I wanted to join the Marine Corps. Therefore, I opted not to enroll for my sophomore year. Instead, I joined my father working in the shipyards from the end of my freshman year at the university until I entered the service of our country.

CHAPTER II - WORLD WAR II - 1942 TO 1946

THE MARINE CORPS CALLS

Having decided which branch of the military in which I wanted to serve, in early fall of 1943 I visited the Marine Corps recruiting center in San Francisco. I told the recruiting officer that I wanted to join with only one request. Inasmuch as my birthday is on December 17, I requested that I not be ordered to report for active duty until after Christmas so I could enjoy the upcoming holiday season with my family. I felt that there was no way of knowing how long it might be until we would be together again. I was assured that my request would be honored. I signed the enlistment documents in high spirits.

It was not too long thereafter that I received a registered letter ordering me to report for induction on December 17, my eighteenth birthday. So much for verbal promises in a time of crisis! While I was personally disappointed, I felt especially sorry for my mother. As she read the letter she knew that the life of our closely-knit family had changed abruptly from a life of peacetime security into a life of wartime uncertainty.

The morning of December 17 was departure day. Mom and Pop drove me from our home in Alamo across the shimmering San Francisco Bay into the heart of the city. Quickly we said our sad goodbyes outside of the recruiting station located in the Palace Hotel on lower Market Street. Shortly thereafter five of us held up our right hands and were sworn in I was now officially a member of the United States Marine Corps.

Our first assignment was to swab the deck (mop the floor) of the recruiting office. We were then on our own until that evening when we were ordered to report to the Southern Pacific train depot to board a passenger train for an overnight journey to Los Angeles. We had been told by the recruiting officer that we had sleeper berths. As we walked down the aisle searching for our berths, it was not long before we were abruptly informed by the train's conductor we had seats in a coach car. Again, so much for verbal promises! We arrived at Union Station in Los Angeles after sitting up all night without much, if any, sleep. There we were joined with a contingent of fellow recruits from all parts of the country. It was not long before we boarded another train and were on our way to San Diego.

Several hours later we walked off the train and into a whole new world. Seasoned Marines in immaculately starched uniforms brusquely ordered us to form into some semblance of rank. We then boarded waiting busses and were transported to the Marine Corps Base.

We had suddenly and effectively left our civilian status behind us.

The Marine Corp indoctrination program is known as a boot camp. At that time it consisted of a twelve-week period of vigorous basic training. The Marine Corps boot camp was recognized among all branches of the military service as the most demanding of all basic training programs. The drill instructors in the Marine Corps were extremely tough taskmasters. "Boots" were trained to give unquestioned obedience to all orders given them by superior officers. As one drill instructor so succinctly told us: "we don't run this outfit by committees." There was a single purpose to this strict regimen. That was to transform raw recruits from carefree young civilians into disciplined proud Marines.

By the time we had finished basic training we were prepared to move on to wherever our orders directed us. Many of my fellow boot camp graduates were immediately assigned to the Third, Fourth and Fifth Marine Divisions as combat infantrymen. Others were ordered to report for specialty training. I was selected to attend radio operator's school located at an area adjacent to the recruit training facility on the same base in San Diego. This was a fortunate transfer as future events would reveal. The school consisted of learning how to send and receive the international code (Morse code) of dots and dashes.

At the conclusion of basic radio school, most newly trained radiomen were immediately deployed overseas and assigned to Marine assault force units scattered throughout the Pacific theater of operations. I was placed with a small group to await transfer to Omaha, Nebraska to learn how to become a radio technician. While waiting for this transfer, word was received that the school was inactivated. Most of us in that group were immediately reassigned to overseas units also.

Once again, good fortune was with me. I remained on the base and was selected to receive additional training at the High Speed Radio Operator School. It was located at the same training facility from which I had matriculated a short time earlier as an apprentice radio operator. At the High Speed Radio School, the field condition training utilizing a writing pad on the knee with a radio pack on your back was replaced by typewriters in front of short-wave radios with earphones. We were now challenged to learn to send and receive code up to three or four times the speed that we had attained at the basic radio operator school.

In retrospect, this experience added another valuable contribution to a lifelong exposure to the importance of the character development processes. In addition to forcing one to constantly try to master sending and receiving code at ever faster speeds, the school created within its trainees the satisfaction of knowing that persistence has its rewards. Oftentimes we would hit a speed wall that we could not immediately penetrate. Through personal persistence and the encouragement of our instructors we would ultimately succeed in knocking it down and move ahead to the next barrier. There was always an emotional high when what was perceived as an absolute limit was permeated through desire and practice. Throughout my lifetime, examples of such persistence in other arenas could very well be traced back to one young Marine's determination to succeed at this challenging school.

An interesting sidelight to this year of basic and advanced training in San Diego was that we were granted occasional weekend passes to be away from the base. It was approximately 350 miles from San Diego to our home in Kingsburg. There was no train or bus service available that would permit traveling so far in such a short period of time. Non-military air travel was non-existent. Hitchhiking was the accepted mode of transfer for enlisted military personnel. Every three or four weeks I would leave the base after Saturday morning inspection (usually about 10 a.m.) and stand alongside the nearby highway with my thumb extended. Beside me would be dozens of other Marine and Naval personnel. Most were seeking rides to the Los Angeles area. It is to the credit of those driving automobiles (primarily civilians) that almost no one who had an available passenger seat in their vehicle would pass by a service man needing a ride.

After traveling through the maze of the Los Angeles basin, over the surrounding mountains and descending into the great San Joaquin Valley, I would normally arrive in Kingsburg as dusk approached. What a joy it was to spend the rest of Saturday evening, Sunday morning and early afternoon with my parents and brothers. About 2 p.m. on Sunday afternoon it would be time to reverse the process. I had been home about twenty hours. We would all go together the few blocks to the southbound highway. After hugs and goodbyes I would stand by the road and hoist my thumb. It was not long before a car would stop and I would begin the long trek back to San Diego. By 6 a.m. on Monday morning I would be back on the base ready to resume my duties.

As I look back on these long trips made possible by the generosity of patriots with automobiles, I sense that ingrained in all of this process was a tacit understanding that sharing is a vital part of life. In the World War II era, giving a serviceman a ride was as an expression of appreciation for their service and sacrifice. With others it might be the sharing of one's time and financial resources in support of the Red Cross or similar agencies. In this great country, good people, in times of stress reached out to each other. These attributes continued as a vital component of the nation's psyche toward returning service personnel when the war was over.

Mid-December 1944, would see my last weekend hitchhiking trip to Kingsburg for many months. While I think that my parents sensed that I was soon to be sent overseas (and I was sure of it), this discussion did not arise during the scant hours that I was home. When I waved goodbye to my brothers and parents that Sunday afternoon shortly before Christmas, it was a time of wondering what the future would bring and when and if I would ever see them again.

Assignment Pearl Harbor

January 3, 1945, was my departure day from San Diego. I joined hundreds of Marines carrying sea bags crammed with all of our possessions, boarding the trucks and busses that transported us from our pre-embarkation base at Camp Pendleton to the San Diego pier. As our names were called while we stood in ranks on the dock, we hoisted our sea bags over our shoulders and walked up the steep gangway of the awaiting troop ship. We immediately faced aft, saluted the flag on its stern, and proceeded into the troop compartments of the vessel. Our canvas bunks were stacked six high. There was barely enough vertical space between them to allow one to turn over without one's shoulder scraping the body of the person in the bunk above. Once at sea we began a constant zigzag course designed to thwart any attack by a Japanese submarine. At night we were under an absolute blackout for the same reason.

Six days later we arrived within the security of the crystal clear waters off of Oahu. For most of the Marines aboard it was our first sea voyage. As we neared the semi-tropical shoreline, the sparkling blue-green waters inside the island's protective coral reef coupled with the swaying palm trees of the lush green hillsides created movie induced mental expectations of sarong-clad islanders running along the sandy beach to greet us. So much for movie induced mental expectations! What awaited us was the bustling city of Honolulu surrounded by military and civilian compounds all directed at supporting this Pacific Ocean outpost of the United States of America.

However, it is proper to comment that in subsequent vacation trips to the Hawaiian Islands in the many intervening years, a charming naturalness is still there for those for those who search it out. To discover it is to move away from the elaborate resort hotels, wall-to-wall shops, crowded highways and lush golf courses and seek out the secluded beaches, back roads, gushing streams, stunning waterfalls, and quiet villages.

My first overseas assignment was as a radioman at Marine Corps Headquarters, Pacific, located within Pearl Harbor. Our billet was at Camp Catlin located about five miles away. Our work schedule was staggered so that we would work around the clock over a period of three days. Because of this, we were free from having to stand routine inspections. We were likewise free to leave the camp when not on duty. For a private first class, it was a great job.

My duty as high-speed radio operator was to sit in front of a typewriter with headphones and type coded messages for periods of from three to five hours per shift. Most messages originated in Washington, D.C. It was a monotonous but demanding assignment. We had no knowledge of the information contained in what we were receiving. We would give the messages to the decoders in the connecting Quonset hut who would unscramble the five letter blocks into a readable message. Most were of a very sensitive nature. The only deviation would be an occasional message transmitted in English.

One lasting memory of receiving an English message was when I typed a bulletin from Secretary of the Navy James Forestall. The Secretary informed us that President Franklin D. Roosevelt had just died and that Vice-President Harry S. Truman had been sworn in to replace him. President Roosevelt had just begun his thirteenth year (fourth term) as President.

It was also during my assignment here that we received word that Germany and Italy had surrendered. The war in Europe was over. Now all focus could be on bringing the war against Japan to an end as rapidly as possible.

A second memorable occasion, which had nothing directly to do with my assigned tasks, was when word arrived that the first contingent of lady Marines had arrived on the island. Several of them were assigned to our communications contingent and became very proficient at their work. Other than Navy and Army nurses, female members of the armed forces were prohibited from being assigned to active combat positions throughout the war.

It was not long after the lady Marines arrived that four of my buddies with whom I had trained in San Diego, were transferred elsewhere. I was the only one to remain at Pearl Harbor. One day I asked our sergeant why they were leaving and I was remaining. His answer was astonishingly simple. He said: "I have to manually type all of the transfer orders so I picked the four guys with the shortest names."

During the time that I was assigned to Marine Corps Headquarters, the fierce battle for the far Pacific island of Iwo Jima was being waged. The invasion consisting of 74,000 Marines was launched on February 19. The time projected to occupy and secure the island was a week or less. What was not projected was the fighting force of approximately 21,000 Japanese embedded deeply within the caves throughout the island. The first day resulted in 2,400 American casualties. By the time the battle was over five weeks later, a total of almost 25,000 Marines, sailors, and soldiers had died or been wounded. Almost all of the Japanese defenders had lost their lives, preferring Hara Kari (suicide) to surrender and capture.

At the battle's conclusion the participating Marine Divisions returned to their home bases. Among them was the Fourth Marine Division which was stationed on the nearby island of Maui. The Fifth Division had its permanent base on the island of Hawaii. The island of Kauai also was home to another contingent of Marines.

By early summer an order was received that all Marines who had not experienced combat operations were to be reassigned to a line organization. Now it was my turn too, long last name or not!

The Fourth Marine Division, Maui

In early summer I boarded the inter-island ferry for the overnight boat trip to Maui. Once there I joined the Fourth Marine Division Joint Assault Signal Company. As earlier noted, the division had only recently returned from Iwo Jima after losing over one-third of its complement killed or wounded. In short order replacements had to be trained and integrated into the units of those who had returned as quickly as possible.

It was soon apparent to me that there was no self-glorification among the survivors. I had joined a group of heroes. They had not only accomplished the successful invasion and capture of Iwo Jima but many of them were also veterans of the earlier victories in the battles of Saipan and Tinian in the Marshall Islands. I do not think that today's generation can grasp the immensity of these tide-turning battles. Lovely tropical islands bordered by stunning white sand beaches became blood soaked battlefields crowded with men and machines engaged in a life and death struggle for survival until victory was achieved.

Special note should be made that the Marine Corps did not posses a medical component. Navy Corpsmen are assigned to fulfill that duty. My cousin Robert Brewer was a Navy Corpsman assigned to the Fourth Marine Division and participated in the battle for Iwo Jima as well as Saipan and Tinian. These brave medics wore Marine Corps uniforms and went ashore in the same landing craft as did the combat Marines. They were highly skilled specialists with a passion for tending to the battlefield needs of those wounded in the line of duty. It was very special to spend time with Robert while we were both stationed on Maui.

Living among combat veterans of the Fourth Marine Division in their rest and recuperation encampment on Maui was in stark contrast to the relatively comfortable conditions I had enjoyed on Oahu. For the six months that I was stationed there, we lived in tents. We had pit toilets. We took cold showers. We had no hot water except for those who wished an allotted "one helmet per person" for shaving purposes. To obtain this small allotment of hot water one had to walk to the mess tent a quarter of a mile away. Travel on occasional off duty passes to the towns of Makawao, Wailuku, or Lahaina was accomplished by riding on a bench seat in the rear of a bouncing military 6 x 6 truck along bumpy roads, choking in the thick red dust of the surrounding pineapple and sugar cane fields.

Overriding all of these annoying discomforts, however, was a sense of camaraderie among the Marines stationed there. New arrivals were accepted without discrimination. There was little or no talk of the Division's past experiences. The focus was on continuing training for what everyone knew would be our next and final assault—the invasion of the islands of Japan. As summer dragged into autumn, the combat training intensified. Our unit worked through numerous exercises in the dense rain forests on the Hana side of the island as well in the cactus and sagebrush near Wailea. Our task was to become as proficient as possible in setting up communication command posts.

In a combat operation, the specific purpose of the Joint Assault Signal Company to which I was assigned was to be the first communications unit sent ashore. It would be our task to set up a radio communications network on the beach. It goes without saying that anyone carrying a large radio backpack made an inviting target for shore-based defenders. There was a feeling among those Marines who had experienced these pre-departure exercises before earlier assaults, that our time for departure was close at hand.

The heroes that survived these ferocious island battles came home with inner scars and inspiring memories that will always be within them. Such is the valor of those who comprise the "Greatest Generation." It was an honor to serve among them if only for a relatively brief period of time. While our Marine Corps indoctrination and "esprit de corps" always stressed our motto, it was here that I began to grasp a full understanding of "Semper Fidelis."

The Fighting is Over!

In October 1945, a major page in world history was written! An atomic bomb was dropped on Hiroshima, Japan. An entire city was destroyed in seconds. Two days later a second bomb was dropped on Nagasaki with a similar result. Immediately, the Japanese high command made arrangements to surrender. Suddenly the most far-flung and expensive war in history was over. At our base there was a tremendous celebration of thanksgiving throughout the camp. In one ecstatic moment the constant worry of the Marines stationed there was gone. No longer did we face the specter of an expected loss of life predicted to make previous invasions pale in comparison. Almost overnight, the elation centered around who would get to go home and how soon. It was out of the ranks of members of this Marine Division and others like them scattered throughout the world that the Greatest Generation was defined. Within these men and women there existed an appreciation for our nation and a pride in what it had accomplished.

With the support of all of those serving on the home front, the United States Armed Forces, in conjunction with our allies, had defeated three of the existing major despotic threats to the democratic societies of the world. It must be remembered that countries besides our own had lost territory to the Axis nations. In Europe entire nations had been overrun by the German armies. In the Pacific numerous nations had lost territory to the Japanese, beginning with their invasion of the Shantung Peninsula on the mainland of northern China as early as 1933. Our nation's major losses were the Philippine Islands, Samoa, Guam, and Attu in the Aleutian Islands of Alaska. Great Britain and France had lost territory in Southeast Asia including Singapore. Australia and New Zealand had lost numerous island territories in the South Pacific. The flag of the Rising Sun had flown over a vast area.

The only damper on this tremendous victory was that future problems still remained in our relationship with our tenuous wartime ally, the Soviet Union. Under Stalin's leadership, the Russians had freed a number of east European democratic nations from the grasp of Hitler's Germany only to drape them in darkness under the oppression of the USSR's Iron Curtain. The fact that the tyranny of the Soviet Union would one day be overcome may be, in large degree, credited to the perseverance of those who lived through the World War II experience. It is fair to say that those who lived through the trauma of World War II came away with a keener real world understanding of the significance of "freedom and justice for all."

Reassignment - Guam

Within sixty days of the Japanese surrender aboard the battleship USS Missouri in Tokyo Bay, the Fourth Marine Division was on its way to dissolution as an effective fighting force. A point system was established to determine who would go home and who would remain overseas. Points were allotted for months overseas and for the number of days in combat. All of those who had served in combat were automatically sent back to the States for discharge or reenlistment at their choice. Others who had not been in combat situations or did not have enough months overseas to be eligible to return home, were placed on standby status to await further word as to our new assignments.

In my case, by the end of November, I found myself aboard an LST for a bouncy all day voyage from Maui back to Pearl Harbor. Once there I was transferred to an aircraft carrier from which all planes had been removed so that cots could be set up in the hanger deck. That night the newly configured "troop" ship began a ten day east-bound voyage to the tiny island of Guam. This time we sailed in a straight line with all lights shining.

Upon debarking at Guam, I was based at a transient tent city some miles removed from the capital city of Agana. Fierce battles against the invading Japanese forces had been fought here early in the war. As a result, other than coconut trees, Agana had nothing taller than five feet of rubble. We were all cautioned that the jungle still contained isolated Japanese soldiers who had not yet surrendered. Today, a rebuilt Guam is once again a vibrant territory of this nation. It is also a major tourist center for visiting Japanese vacationers.

The climate on Guam is a combination of searing heat and stifling humidity. My assignment while awaiting further orders was to take a physical inventory of the base tents every day to see how many were in use and the number of Marines billeted in each. It was a "make work" project at best. All tasks were carried out as early as possible in the morning in order to do as little as possible in the punishing mid-day heat. While I was on Guam I had my first opportunity to see a B29 bomber up close and personal. This is the same type of plane that dropped the atom bombs on Hiroshima and Nagasaki only a few months earlier. My wide-eyed reaction was simply to question to how such a large airplane could ever leave the ground!

Tsingtao China

By mid-December some of us were issued cold weather clothing and told we were being reassigned to Tsingtao (now Chingdao), China, on the underside of the Shantung Peninsula near Peking (now Beijing). Japan's military aggressiveness had really started here in 1933. We were informed that we would be assigned to the Sixth Marine Division whose job it was to repatriate the Japanese military back to their homeland.

Almost overnight, on our sea voyage north we experienced a climate change from the stifling heat of the equator to the chilling temperatures of the sub-arctic. We docked in Tsingtao on a cold blustery mid-winter day. As soon as we were ashore, we were transported through the city to our new quarters located in the converted classrooms of an appropriated school building. I was assigned to the Division's communication center formerly occupied by the

Japanese. It was located in an impressive ship-shaped building on the waterfront.

After only a week or so at this assignment, I was transferred again. My new assignment was as news editor for Armed Forces radio station XABU, "The Voice of the Marines." My job was to obtain the news via short wave radio from the United States and then edit what I had received into a script for airing by the station's announcers. Our audience consisted primarily of Marines and Navy personnel stationed in that area either ashore or on naval vessels in port.

For the next nine months I lived a life of relative luxury with a complement of twelve other Marines in a private home/studio. At one time we had a total of twelve Chinese houseboys assigned to our unit. Among them we had a cook, a custodian, a waiter, a room attendant, even a young man whom we dubbed "keeper of the flame" whose job it was to keep the charcoal fire burning under a water barrel so that we would have hot water.

While there are many stories that could be told about this period of my life, perhaps the most noteworthy was being forewarned that radio communication from the United States would be disrupted for a period of time on a particular day. That prediction proved to be totally true. I shall always remember it. A test was made of an atomic bomb being dropped on a tiny atoll in the Bikini Islands. As predicted, the force of the blast totally disrupted radio communications throughout the Pacific Ocean region. For at least a day it was impossible to receive a radio signal. There was no current news from home for our newscasts. My skills at rewriting old scripts to make them sound like fresh news when read by our announcers were sorely tested.

One of my additional duties was to operate the movie projectors at our little theatre on the rooftop of our building. Within Tsingtao was a large Catholic Cathedral. The lieutenant in charge of our unit, a Catholic, became acquainted with the presiding Bishop. One evening he arranged for a visit to our radio station by several priests accompanied by five or six nuns. The movie I had selected for that night was Bing Crosby's immortal "Going My Way." It was an evening of great joy watching these devoted men and women sit on our rooftop and have a carefree few hours. I wondered that night and have wondered many times since how long it had been since these priests and nuns had seen an American movie. I have often wondered what became of them after the Communists gained control of that country in 1949.

Finally in August 1946, not quite one year after the war with Japan had formally ceased, I received word that I was going home. Boarding my last troop ship for the long journey back to the United States was an emotional experience. As we sailed away from Tsingtao, it was with the realization that my life's journey would never bring me here again. After docking in Tsiensen to pick up a contingent of returning Marines who had been stationed in Peking, we were, at last, on the long non-stop voyage back to San Diego.

After lunch on the second day at sea, I went on deck to watch as we passed by the southern coast of Honshu Island. Rumor had it that this is where the Fourth Marine Division was scheduled to go ashore, had the war not ended. As I watched, the weather became more and more severe. Before nightfall we were in the middle of a tremendous storm and the six thousand returning troops aboard were ordered to remain below deck. The violent weather lasted three full days with the ship being tossed in all directions. At its abatement we were once again allowed up on deck. However, the entire remaining voyage saw the ship traveling at a reduced speed and listing slightly to starboard.

Sixteen days after leaving Tsingtao I stood at the ship's railing in the early pre-dawn darkness and was filled with thanksgiving as the lights of the San Diego coastline came slowly into view. I had spent forty-five days of my life at sea on a grand circle of the Pacific. Over a year and a half after sailing into the vastness of the Pacific Theater of Operations, I was safely home.

Three days later I had my discharge papers as a Corporal in the United States Marine Corps. In late afternoon I picked up my sea bag, threw it over my shoulder, and walked outside the base gate for the last time. Once again I stood alongside the familiar highway and hitchhiked my final long ride home to that beautiful little city - Kingsburg, California.

Early on an August 1946 morning, after hitchhiking all night, I walked from the busy highway down the quiet small-town street to our modest home. First to recognize me was our dog, Rex. In a way that only a dog could explain, Rex spotted me while I was still several hundred yards from home. He could hardly contain his joy as he came running and leaping toward me. Who would believe that this little dog could remember someone after so many months?

Next to greet me was my mother. She was out in her yard, watering her very special geranium plants to protect them from the oppressive midday valley heat of late summer. What a joy it was to hug her and hold her close. Her daily letters to me often came in bunches; but there was indescribable comfort in knowing that even though we may have been separated by earthly distances, we were never apart in our love for each other.

Life consists of memories like these - never to be forgotten. These few moments were but two of them.

A chapter in my life was closing. It was now time to reenter the civilian world of folks who appreciate this great country and endure those who do not. There was no question in my mind where I stood.

War Time Reflections

The observations described above are not offered from an avid academic desire to understand sociology or record historical events. Rather, they arise from the impressions of a twenty-year old Marine Private First Class going about his assigned duties. It is with a sense of excitement that this period of reflection arises anew, some sixty years later. It is my purpose to weave these wartime recollections into the context of this personal travelogue as we retrace a lifelong journey.

Mr. Brokaw, in his book of tribute to my generation, included service in the armed forces during World War II as an implied qualification for full equity membership. I would submit that we not forget all of those who labored so diligently in the civilian arena to support those in uniform. Theirs was a special contribution to a global conflict. In saying that, it is nevertheless proper that I reflect upon the aspects of my Marine Corp experience and how those months of military service affected me in subsequent years. It is helpful that we recognize that we are deeply influenced by a montage of experience over which we often had little or no control. The discipline of Marine regimen, the pride of the Corps, the appreciation of country, the dependence upon one another for survival, the support of family and friends back home, and the acknowledgment of a Supreme God, are but some of the foundation blocks upon which my memories are built.

Separation from family and friends and the longing to be with them were inevitable. While there was time for self-pity if one dwelled upon it, one's daily activities crowded out such thoughts for the most part. That did not preclude staying in touch as much as possible. As often as I could find the time, I would write a letter to my family. When writing from overseas, we used a special very light tissue paper called "V-mail". All overseas letters written by enlisted personnel were censored by commissioned officers for content until the end of the war. We could not describe where we were or specifically what we were doing. I am sure my letters became very repetitious. The primary purpose was to let the folks back home know that all was well. As I continue to recreate this lifelong journey, nearby is a box in which my mother saved every one of the letters I wrote during those many months when I was away.

On the West Coast of the United States particularly, following the attack on Pearl Harbor, all Japanese-Americans were judged by our semi-traumatized government officials to be individuals not to be trusted. In the ensuing days and weeks these hardworking members of our society were quickly removed from their residences, farms, and businesses. They were initially relocated into hastily assembled in-transit camps such as local racetracks, fairgrounds, etc. From these temporary accommodations it was not long before they were sent to more permanent penal-type locations away from the coastline. There they remained until the war was over and they were permitted to return.

There is an ironic and heroic sidebar to this miscarriage of "justice for all". Many young Japanese-Americans enlisted in the United States Army directly from the internment camps. They formed a brigade of soldiers and were ultimately assigned to fight against the Italians and Germans primarily in northern Italy. That brigade became the most decorated unit in the United States Army.

I remember my special Japanese-American friend in high school telling me one time that the worst thing a child of Japanese ancestry could do is to disgrace one's parents through personal misconduct. Today, in the early 21st century which includes gangs, dope, and corporate crimes of greed, it is almost impossible to cite an instance in which one of today's Japanese-American men or women is involved.

A final thought about the toxic nature of racial profiling is the profound impression I received upon arrival in the Hawaiian Islands. A large percentage of the population was comprised of people of Japanese heritage. Even though the Hawaiian Islands were still a territory and not a state, those who resided there were intensely loyal to the United States of America. To my knowledge, there was not one serious instance of any subversive act by any person of Japanese ancestry in those beautiful islands during World War II.

Another impression that I carried away from the Hawaiian Islands also involved the absence of bigotry. Intermarriage was common. Polynesians, Asians, and Caucasians mingled freely as they went about their daily lives. At first it was a novelty to see the interaction, dating, and multi-racial families among the residents of Hawaii. Those of us coming from a different cultural background learned, after only a few months, that it was completely expected to accept people without scrutiny as to national origin or religious affiliation.

Looking back upon that scenario from today's vantage point, I think that many of my generation have a broader understanding of the real meaning of tolerance because of our time among the Islanders. Such understanding has remained within our psyches because we had the opportunity to personally witness the openness of societal love without racial, religious, or cultural prejudice.

Accentuating the cultural democracy of the Islands was the contrasting situation that awaited us upon our return to the mainland of America. At the war's end, our nation still accepted racial segregation as a fact of life primarily throughout the southern states. African-Americans rode in the back of busses. They attended inferior and racially segregated schools. People worshipped a common God but in separate churches. This country still had community pockets of ethnic and religious neighborhoods populated by recent arrivals from countries such as China, Italy, Germany, Ireland, Armenia and yes, even Sweden. Socialization was passively permissible but intermarriage was socially taboo. In many aspects, our nation was a melting pot that had become stagnant, separated, and congealed.

China and its multitudes also made a lasting impression upon me, but in a different way. That great nation was about to be taken over by the Communists in 1933, when the Japanese invaded the Shantung Peninsula. This war action derailed the impending Chinese Communist insurgency and reunited China under the authoritarian and corrupt government of Chiang Kai-shek.

Upon arriving in north China in late 1945, the most dramatic illustration I witnessed of the ongoing misconduct of the Nationalist government was the dramatic gap between the "haves" and the "have nots." The wealthy rode about the city in elaborate rickshaws pulled by human animals days or hours away from starvation. Emaciated women and children were everywhere, gauntly seeking to gather straw and branches to enable them to boil scarce rice over an open fire. These people were on opposite ends of their economic world. Several of the Chinese men who were working at our radio station were members of wealthy families from inland areas. They had fled to Tsingtao to escape from the Communists who were already taking over outlying cities. As part of the formerly elite, these now desperate émigrés within their own country were destined for execution if captured by the Communists.

During my last months in that city, we could hear the shelling on the outskirts between the Nationalists and the Communists. The presence of United States military personnel within the city itself was the only deterrent to the fighting entering its boundaries. I remember thinking that if I were one of the maligned poor in this country, I would be sorely tempted to support the Communist uprising. Perhaps it is out of this experience that I retain such a passion to elect a compassionate government run by properly motivated public servants. No one should be without hope in this bountiful land. Our generation has subscribed to these ideals with intermittent successes. It is up to those who will follow to continue the quest.

A final thought on this highly influential period of my life; it was a time during which our country was united in defending itself from the holocaust of world-wide subjugation to the tyrannical dictates of an evil alliance of despots. It took an "act of infamy" to awaken our nation to the devastation of war. It took an "era of family" to permit us to attain an eventual triumph.

It is not surprising that the infinite sacrifices that took place during the four years of worldwide turmoil from 1941 until 1945, have become no more than a chapter in our history books studied by today's youth. Many of the details surrounding this great effort have become blurred with the passage of time. It is my deepest hope and prayer, however, that the lessons learned in tolerance, fairness, compassion, freedom, and justice never be removed from the fabric of this great land from the daily lives and minds of its people.

CHAPTER III - 1946 TO 1971

A CIVILIAN AGAIN

My hometown, Kingsburg, is in the heart of the raisin producing area of California. At the time of my discharge from the Marine Corps in August 1946, grape harvest was in full swing. Lush, ripe Thompson Seedless grapes are picked by hand and placed on paper trays between the rows of vines to dry. About half way through this process, the trays upon which the grapes are drying need to be turned over. This requires two people who have the stamina to work bent at the waist all day in the late summer heat. College did not start for another month. To earn some quick money I accepted the invitation of a former high school classmate, who had only recently been discharged from the Army, to be his partner turning trays. He already had verbal contracts with several vineyard owners. We had both forgotten that it takes a special set of well conditioned muscles to work stooped over all day long. We quickly learned that there is a vast chasm between being militarily fit and "tray turning" fit. Payment is based upon the number of trays turned. I lasted three days. My friend wound up in the hospital from heat exhaustion. The moral of this story: Be sure you are really ready to get to work - don't accept tasks which you are not prepared to handle.

At the war's conclusion, Congress passed what came to be known at the "GI Bill of Rights." Its purpose was to assist the transition of discharged military men and women back into a productive civilian life. One of the features of this bill was that the government would pay for college tuition, pay an allowance for books, and provide a monthly stipend for incidental living expenses. About the same time that I joined the Marine Corps, my parents and brothers moved back to Kingsburg from their two year residence in the San Francisco Bay area. Inasmuch as I had been away from home for quite some time, I opted to attend nearby Reedley College for my sophomore year rather than immediately go away again to continue my education in Berkeley. This single decision would have a tremendous impact upon the rest of my life.

Reedley College was a small two-year Community College with intimate sized classes and an accessible faculty. It was a vivid contrast to my collegiate freshman experience at the University of California where my first Economics class had more students than the entire high school from which I had recently graduated. At Reedley College each student had an opportunity to become a recognizable personality. One of my lasting impressions upon returning to a smaller college was realizing the almost unfair advantage that we returning service men and women had over those entering college directly from high school. We knew why we were there. We were focused on our future.

We knew the value of study. We appreciated the value of higher education. We were profoundly thankful for this educational opportunity.

May 1947 was cap and gown time during which we were presented with our Associate of Arts degrees. I had the good fortune to sit beside a girl whom I had seen around the campus during the school year but never knew very well. Her right arm was in a sling as she had recently slipped on some wet pavement and dislocated her elbow. One warm July afternoon, my buddy and I were passing some time chatting in the city park in Kingsburg. I casually asked him what he thought about us calling the girl I sat next to on graduation night. I suggested asking her if she would like to invite a friend and the four of us would go to Fresno to see a movie. I was aware that my friend knew her much better than I. He agreed. We made the telephone call. She accepted and said she would invite one of her girlfriends to complete our double date group. On the eventful night, my friend Glenn and I drove in my parents' car to her parents' home to pick up the two girls. As fate would have it, her friend got into the backseat with Glenn, and Althea Moran was left with no choice but to get into the front seat with me. It was a fateful decision for both of us.

All through my second year of college at Reedley, I was mentally prepared to return to the University of California at Berkeley to obtain my Bachelor of Arts degree. However, halfway through the spring semester, one of the professors told some of us about a private business school in Berkeley. It had an excellent reputation. The cost to attend was well beyond what I could afford but the provisions of the GI Bill made it possible to overcome that obstacle. I applied for admittance and was accepted. So, rather than returning to UC Berkeley, I enrolled at Armstrong University. The student body was composed almost entirely of veterans. The courses were very intense. The instructors were primarily private sector men and women who had become full or part-time faculty members after successful careers in the business world. By going without a summer break, combined with a heavy unit load, I was able to obtain my Bachelor of Business Administration degree in December 1948.

If there is a characteristic that I and so many others like myself took away from this period of our lives, it was an awareness that relevancy is the key component to education. Understanding how obtaining knowledge can be as practical as eating breakfast makes everything come together. As the years have passed, I have realized that this rationale applies at all educational levels and is not confined solely to higher education. I cannot close out this portion of my life without commenting upon the generosity of our nation, by providing special legislation to assist veterans of World War II with their financial needs upon their discharge from military duty. Without it, my life would surely have traveled a much different course.

A CAREER BEGINS

And so it came to pass that I began the year of 1949 in my first full time post-college civilian job with my brand new degree certifying that I was a "major expert" in the field of merchandising and a "minor expert" in the field of advertising. I reported for work at Sun-Maid Raisin Growers of California in Fresno on January 2nd. While they did not have an immediate opening in their marketing department, they did have an office full of gray beards so I accepted an interim position assisting their employment manager. It is interesting to reflect that women were not a factor in filling management positions in 1948. They worked as receptionists, in the bookkeeping department, and as secretaries. Being executive secretary to the president or general manager was an ultimate position for a woman.

Only a few months later I was assigned to work with the traffic manager in Sun-Maid's logistics (called "transportation" at that time) department. Once again a strange twist of fate determined my life's journey. My boss, the traffic manager, liked the work that I was doing. He went out of his way to encourage me. Learning the intricacies of shipping a product anywhere in the world by railcar, truck, or ship fascinated me. The logistics business became my passion and has remained so for all of my working life.

In June of that year, Althea and I were wed in the United Presbyterian Church in the small town of Easton. We rented an old home in the center of Fresno for $27.50 per month. I was earning a base salary of $175 a month plus another $25 a month for working a half day each Saturday.

Herein may lay a fundamental characteristic of our generation. As kids, we knew the tribulations of the Great Depression. As military personnel, we knew the restrictions of living on a monthly income beginning at $21 per month. Frugality was an ingrained way of life except for the privileged few. Wasteful spending was abhorrent, whether governmental or personal. Credit cards were non-existent. Loans were reserved primarily for automobiles and homes. Families were close and friendships were meaningful and lasting. Watching TV had not yet replaced chatting with one's neighbors or, alas, one's own family members. Life moved at what seemed to be a bit slower and more meaningful pace. With the love and support of our parents, Althea and I entered into a life-long partnership that is now into its sixth decade.

In October 1950, tragedy struck our family. Across the street from our family home in Kingsburg was a business that made cement conduits used in sewer lines, irrigation fields, etc. Within the facility was a pit into which sand was stored until needed. Normally the sand was delivered by trailers that were emptied by opening doors in their bottoms. Walter, my youngest brother who was seven, liked to cross the street and watch the trucks deliver the sand despite my parents telling him not to do so. On this particular day, the truck delivering the sand had a trailer that rose from the front and the sand slid out the rear. Walter was standing immediately behind the trailer when the sand came down on him. It was several hours before his small hand was discovered sticking out of the sand pile.

The stress that fell upon my mother and father was almost unbearable. Paul, my oldest brother, was attending the University of California in Berkeley, preparing to enter the UC Medical School in San Francisco. Howard, my middle brother, was attending Reedley College and was still residing at home. It was he who bore the day-to-day pain of watching our parents suffer through the loss of their little boy. The outpouring of love and support from the community, friends, and particularly from the members of the Holy Name Catholic Church, provided an indescribable source of reassurance that helped my mom and dad survive this family tragedy.

After four years of employment with the raisin packing company, an opportunity to focus solely within the transportation field arose. I resigned from Sun-Maid Raisin Growers to accept a position with a transportation brokerage firm. This was done with some delicacy as my former employer, Sun-Maid, was the largest account of my new employer. It was to the credit of the Sun-Maid traffic manager under whom I worked, that he encouraged me to accept the new job offer so I could concentrate on the logistical side of the business world. I left with the good wishes of the Sun-Maid administrative staff.

At 8 o'clock on the morning of January 2, 1953, I was scheduled to report for my first day of work at California Trucking Exchange. However, I didn't show up on time. Instead, I was forced to make a telephone call advising my new boss that I would be late for work because Althea was delivering our first-born. Our son, Larry, arrived at 7 a.m. that morning in the same hospital where his dad was born twenty-eight years earlier. Unlike today, when a significant friend, family member or dad can visit the delivery room to participate in the proceedings, at that time only doctors and nurses participated. Expectant fathers waited in the lobby for someone to come and tell them the good news of whether they were the parent of a boy or girl. Only then could they have a brief peek at the new arrival. After a five-minute visit with Althea while she was being wheeled from the delivery room into a hospital room for the mandatory three-day stay, I was off to work—two hours late. I happily gave away the traditional cheap cigars as a proud new father.

As new parents, we had arranged for an elderly lady to come and stay with us for three or four days immediately after Althea returned home from the hospital. She came strongly recommended as she supplemented her modest retirement income by helping new mothers adjust to their first few days with a new baby. Unfortunately, Larry was born with a severe case of colic. Not only did he cry constantly but the doctor could not find a milk formula that agreed with him. Instead of the planned three or four days, the lovely Mrs. Stahl stayed on with us for six weeks. One evening I arrived home from work to find all three of them crying from exhaustion.

At the end of the sixth week, the doctor placed Larry in the newly opened Valley Children's Hospital for observation and treatment. He remained there for five days. When he returned home we awoke one morning in a state of semi-panic realizing that Larry (and Althea and me) had slept through the entire night. At long last we had a baby who was not in constant pain.

Some time later my parents told us of the seriousness of Larry's situation. Paul, my newly licensed doctor brother, told them after a visit that he was very concerned about the chances of Larry surviving. The moral to this episode is to have a child with problems as serious as these - first.

My new job was a perfect fit for me. The transportation brokerage business was relatively new. We were an intermediary service, coordinating the need for interstate truck transportation by shippers and receivers, with the need for cargo by motor carriers. We focused on long haul transportation with three-quarters of the tonnage for which we arranged shipment from California destined to receivers east of the Mississippi River. The Korean War was underway which created a huge imbalance between the amount of westbound manufactured consumer and military goods, and the amount of manufactured products available as tonnage for an eastbound haul. Our company filled that gap by providing eastbound loads of natural farm products such as raisins, nuts, dehydrated vegetables, cotton, and assorted other agricultural products. I liked the challenge of having to assemble differing sized shipments from assorted shippers, combining them into truckloads in such a manner that they could be loaded and unloaded in proper geographical sequence.

As time passed, the map of this country, with all of its highways and cities, became deeply etched into my memory system. An added plus was that my brother, Howard, who was discharged from the U.S. Navy in 1955, had joined the company. The last two years of his enlistment were spent on the island of Guam where I had been stationed briefly almost ten years earlier.

Ours was a business in which integrity was fundamental to lasting success. It was based upon extensive use of the telephone in accepting shipments, offering freight to carriers, and negotiating the freight rate. For that we charged a service fee similar to that of a stockbroker or a real estate broker. One's word that a truck would pick up an order by a certain time, transport it across the country, and deliver it on time for a mutually agreed upon price determined one's stature in the business. Time was of the essence and supporting documents such as freight bills, payments for services, reconciling claims for loss or damage of cargo, always followed the actual verbal transaction.

Unfortunately for the unwary, the unregulated freight brokerage business of that time also consisted of unscrupulous individuals and firms. These unethical leeches oftentimes bilked unsuspecting truckers out of their cartage payments after collecting payment from the shipper or the receiver. The flip side was, of course, that the stronger we established our reputation for fairness and honesty, the more business we handled. More about this later in the journey.

By the middle of 1955, Althea and I exercised another one of our benefits under the GI Bill. We purchased and moved into our own home. A federally insured veteran's home loan was obtainable at an interest rate of 4.5 percent versus 6 percent or higher for a conventional mortgage. We visited a new home development project and excitedly selected our lot and floor plan. A few months later we moved into our very own, newly constructed tract-style home.

It was shortly after moving into our new home that our daughter, Gale, arrived. She ate well. She smiled and laughed rather than writhed and cried. Whereas Larry was always active and into things, Gale was content to sit and play with her dolls and toys. Had their temperaments as newborns been reversed, taking care of Larry would have been even more difficult. Being our first born, we didn't know how wonderful it was to have a baby that didn't scream from pain most of the time he was awake. Conversely, after enduring the difficulties that confronted Larry, we appreciated even more the joy of having a baby with the temperament of Gale.

Our fondest wishes had been granted to us. We had a son and a daughter. We had our family. We had our home. We felt deeply blessed. Little could we anticipate that God had greater earthly blessings in store for us than we could ever have imagined.

Almost all of our new neighbors were young families similar to ours. We quickly developed neighborhood friendships. We planted our lawns and shrubs and seeded our flowerbeds. Soon we were getting together for neighborhood patio parties. We watched out for each other's kids. We took our first steps in learning to become contributors to the community.

THE SEEDS OF STEWARDSHIP

I am convinced that those of us who served this nation during its years of peril came away deeply committed to its ideology. To most of us, such a commitment was articulated through volunteerism. As we became established as a family, it was not long before requests and opportunities arose to begin making contributions of time and substance to community programs.

While I have never been one to seek out places to volunteer my services, I have always tried to assist community-based organizations when approached to do so. To some extent this may have been ingrained into many of us during our military service. No one walked alone. Interdependence was the ultimate resource when times became tough. There was no question about helping one's buddy when help was needed. However, volunteering was often jokingly defined as being involuntarily selected for a specific duty by a superior. There was an adage among all branches of the military service, especially among enlisted personnel, about never raising one's hand even to go to the restroom for fear of being selected for some "volunteer" duty.

Venturing into the area of volunteerism began with a series of both social and business engagements. Becoming a scoutmaster for our son Larry's Boy Scout troop was an exciting early experience in helping kids grow in character and self-confidence. Chaperoning a gaggle of giggling girls in our daughter Gale's Girl Scout troop was also a rich experience. Each of them created an opportunity to develop personal skills while learning the value of social standards. Larry became active in youth baseball. I was asked to become a vice-president of the league. One of my duties was to stroll among five concurrent twilight youth baseball games on a large middle school playground two or three nights a week to make sure all was well. Interestingly, it was not normally the coaches and the players who needed supervision, but overly excited moms and dads who sometimes needed reminding "it was only a game."

In my business world, joining the Fresno Transportation Club and being asked to serve on the board of directors and later as president was a high honor. Representatives of all modes of transportation plus shippers, receivers, and suppliers would meet monthly in a spirit of friendly camaraderie. To be asked by one's peers to lead any professional organization is a great privilege and a rewarding experience.

It was not long before we purchased a small ski boat and joined a local boating club. It was a great family activity and enlarged our circle of friends. Recollections of trips to Lake Millerton and Pine Flat Lake, coupled with an annual weekend outing to the San Joaquin Delta, fill many happy pages in our book of memories. I had the pleasure of serving as Commodore for this fine group of family oriented outdoor enthusiasts.

We were invited to join a dance club appropriately named Los Amigos. With a membership restricted to sixty couples, we would come together once a month to spend an evening dancing to the popular songs of the fifties and sixties. We utilized a facility rented from the Retired Teachers Association and danced to the music of an excellent four-piece band. It was a privilege to serve these friendly folks as their president.

About this same time, the local Council of the Boy Scouts of America asked me to serve in a new capacity. I was asked to review the annual renewal charters for Scout troops and Cub packs. This was a time consuming effort but one that was necessary in order to comply with the regulations of the organization. While most of these charter review meetings were evening affairs, six and a half days away at the office, coupled with being out an evening or two a week with other commitments, began to severely encroach upon any quality time at home with my family.

One evening Althea told me that Larry was very despondent after school that day. When she asked him why, he responded, "Why doesn't dad spend more time at home with us like Ed (the neighbor dad) does with Duane?" The statement struck me like a bolt of lightning. While I believed that my volunteering in various community-based organizations was on behalf of my family, I was stunned to learn that I was actually causing them stress. Needless to say, I took an immediate inventory of my volunteerism. I curtailed some of my activities and became extremely careful with my discretionary time, until Althea and I became empty nesters once again many years later.

Out of this little incident grew an imbedded awareness that there is no more important facet of community stewardship than being a good steward to those one holds most dear. Children are the product of their environment. Special recognition must be given to those caring single parents who are so devoted to their offspring. Far too many of today's children are being raised in broken, non-supportive homes. Lack of parental guidance, parental stewardship if you prefer, is ultimately the root cause of many juvenile problems. The result is a predictable over-taxed human welfare and juvenile justice system.

There was another dynamic that molded my thoughts and actions during the '50s and '60s. Growing up through the Great Depression and surviving service during World War II, I had come to love this country dearly. A great preponderance of veterans returned home with a passion to rebuild the world that we had defended in a massive worldwide struggle at the cost of thousands and thousands of young lives. We came home believing that the United States of America's system of government was the envy of the world.

And that's the way it seemed for awhile. Soon the ugly heads of arrogance, ignorance, and intolerance began to eat away at our personal and collegial dreams. We became exposed to the pettiness of politics. Most of us were too young and otherwise focused before the war began to be involved in political affairs. Most of us came home mature enough to realize that participating in the system was our ultimate responsibility if we were to protect the reemergence of the types of government we had defeated.

A Few Comments on Character

Many of us found it very difficult to observe the difference between those who give of their time and resources unselfishly to help others and those who superficially do so in order to attract attention to themselves. While not exactly a parallel, I believe watching two prominent individuals play out their roles in the immediate postwar years formed the basis for this stark distinction.

When President Franklin Delano Roosevelt died suddenly in 1945, President Harry Truman succeeded him. President Truman, who was then serving as vice-president, was little known to the American people primarily due to the dominant personality of his predecessor. He was a former United States senator from Missouri who operated a haberdashery before entering the political arena. He ascended through the ranks of the Tammany Hall political machine. It was not long, however, before it became evident that this man from the nation's mid-section had within him the qualities demanded of a person in his position as President of the United States of America.

It was President Truman who had the administrative power, and primary historical responsibility to approve use of the first atomic bombs. While they took a terrible toll of human life the two times they were used, it also saved countless Allied lives that would have been lost had an invasion of mainland Japan taken place.

Because he deeply felt the broadest effect of the war and its use of atomic bombs, it was President Truman who initiated the Marshall Plan. This unprecedented post-war program provided relief and reconstruction funds to restore the economies of both our former enemies and our wartime allies. President Truman was a man of immense compassion.

Under President Truman's leadership, nations of the world came together in San Francisco, California and created the United Nations. This new organization was dedicated to insuring that "never again would the world face a global conflagration." While there is much to be done within all areas of the UN charter, our generation deems it worthwhile to speculate on where this world would be today without it.

At President Truman's insistence, the Congress passed legislation limiting the time that anyone may serve as President of the United States to two terms. Upon leaving office, this humble man returned every pencil to the desk of the President and returned, with his devoted wife Bess, to his home state of Missouri. It was there that he spent the rest of his years simply and with dignity.

On the other hand, another popular figure of that time, General Douglas MacArthur, chose a different path. He had developed a strong reputation for military leadership in the Pacific prior to the onset of WWII. He was made the Supreme Commander of all Army forces in the Pacific Theater of Operations immediately after Japan's attack on Pearl Harbor. He accepted the Japanese surrender on the deck of the battleship Missouri in Tokyo Bay at the conclusion of the war. He oversaw the reestablishment of a democratic government in Japan.

During the ensuing Korean War, General MacArthur was placed in charge of all United Nations military forces allied against the invading North Korean army. As the tide of the war turned, the United Nations forces proceeded to rout the North Korean instigators. He exhibited a determination to pursue the fleeing North Korean forces across the Yalu River into Manchuria. Such a drastic action would assuredly have brought the Chinese communist army into the fray.

For his self-centered and self-serving refusal to obey the orders of his Commander-in-Chief and the dictates of the United Nations organization, he was summarily removed of his command by President Truman. He will be remembered as a lonely and broken man.

Two historic figures acted on the world's stage in a starkly differing manner. Each had a role to play and each played it differently.

THE BIG PICTURE FROM A SMALL PERSPECTIVE

If there were a period of greatest influence for the Greatest Generation, I would describe it as those years between the close of World War II through the '60s and

'70s. In the late '40s and into the '50s, there was an air of optimism in the air. A new day was at hand. The world felt safe. A new, more united world was waiting to be formed. There was a euphoric feeling that our nation had overcome a great crisis and that all was well among people of good will. Organizations such as the Peace Corps, the World Health Organization founded by the United Nations, and other similar agencies were focusing on humanitarian needs throughout the world.

The major blight upon this glow of optimism was that we were beginning to realize that significant threats to our democratic way of government still existed. Of most prominence was the increasingly hostile posture of the USSR. Dictatorships still prevailed throughout Africa, Central and South America, Asia, and Europe. Colonialism still existed in such places as India and numerous island states throughout the world. In 1949 China had joined Russia and its subjected states in becoming a communist nation. At the conclusion of the Korean War the fortieth parallel on the Korean peninsula became the dividing line between democratic South Korea and communist North Korea. As time passed we became more and more aware that all was *not* well in the world.

Here at home, President Truman was succeeded in office by former General of the Armies Dwight D. Eisenhower in 1952. While admittedly not a politician, President Eisenhower was a man of strong character.

He was respected throughout the world for his role as Supreme Commander in leading the Allied powers to victory in the European Theatre of Operations in WWII. He had refused to state his preference for a particular political party until a relatively few months before his nomination at the Republican National Convention. His happy grin and ability to relate to all, regardless of social or economic stature, stood him in good stead as he became immersed in the sometimes ugly world of national politics. He was the last president of this great land to propose, enact and *adhere* to a balanced budget. He is also the father of our present interstate highway system.

President Eisenhower was followed by President John F. Kennedy, a Democrat of the first order. John Kennedy came from a long line of strong activists in the Democratic Party. His father had made a fortune during the years that Prohibition was in effect in our land. President Kennedy had a beautiful, young, and talented wife Jackie, the daughter of a prominent Philadelphia family. The two of them were looked upon as the ultimate in sophistication and elegance.

President Kennedy, like so many of his contemporaries, was a naval officer in World War II. He served in the South Pacific as commander of a patrol boat and survived its sinking by enemy gunfire. Under his presidency, this country moved forward with renewed optimism that our future was unfolding as it should. It was this president who fast-forwarded our efforts to explore outer space. It was under his leadership that our nation overtook the Soviets in the space race by placing a man on the moon. It was President Kennedy who went to the brink of nuclear war to persuade the Russians to remove missiles they had installed in Cuba.

It is also historically accurate that it was President Kennedy who committed our first armed forces to the postwar nation of South Vietnam in an effort to counteract the aggressiveness of communist North Vietnam. This quagmire eventually became a national nightmare costing this nation thousands of lives and billions of dollars. It also effectively dimmed the dream of those of us of World War II vintage, that everyone should have the right to choose their own form of government. This nation's inability to protect the independence of South Vietnam was a major emotional setback to those of us who had fought so hard for the sake of worldwide freedom.

Perhaps the most difficult aspect of the Vietnam War became the disillusionment of the younger generation with the aspirations of their seniors. The Viet Nam conflict began under the idealism of protecting freedom for a threatened people. It ended in having the burden of communism forced upon them while our brave service men and women returned home to a hurting and divided country. It is my hope that this book will, in some small way, contribute to the reconciliation of these two strong and dedicated generations.

Our nation suffered a history-altering loss when President Kennedy was assassinated by Lee Harvey Oswald while on a presidential visit to Dallas, Texas. President Lyndon Baines Johnson succeeded President Kennedy. President Johnson was the consummate politician. To his credit it was he who initiated the Great Society program that changed the way that social reform was addressed in this country. However, it was also during his term of office that the Vietnam War escalated dramatically and became extremely unpopular among many American citizens. Young people protested in both conduct and attire. University campuses were magnets for anti-war protests. The ultra-right and the ultra-left engaged in vigorous philosophical debates which oftentimes bordered on self-serving distortions from both sides. Our military forces returned home from the dangers of war without receiving proper recognition for their efforts on behalf of our nation. National morale was at or near an all time low. It was because of this political toxicity that President Johnson declined to seek a second term.

President Richard Nixon, who succeeded Lyndon Johnson, was a blight upon our country. While possessing early popularity, mostly due to disengaging in South Vietnam, it was his paranoiac personality that ultimately brought about his downfall. His first vice-president, Spiro Agnew, was forced to resign for inappropriate personal conduct. His pathetic attempt to steal documents from Democratic Party headquarters in the Watergate Complex was exposed and resulted in the political disgrace and arrest of a number of his high appointees. He secretly taped all conversations held in the Oval Office. He was the only president in our nation's history to be forced to resign from office.

Without continuing this litany of past presidents, I have included those just named because they were our mid-life contemporaries. Each helped form the national backdrop for events that shaped each of our lives as we raised our families, toiled at our jobs and professions, and became part of our local community's efforts to create a better life for all who live, play, work, and pray among us.

A SOCIETY IN TRANSITION

As our children progressed through their grade school years, Althea became actively involved in their classrooms while I helped in after-school activities. Cub Scouts, Brownies, Boy Scouts, and Girl Scouts, all became an integral part of our daily lives. Almost unknowingly by serving as adult leaders, we increased our own awareness of the importance of building character components into the lives of all young people.

As would be expected, by the time our son and daughter entered into high school, their extra curricular interests naturally changed. They became involved in such school related activities as clubs, music, and sports. We were no longer directly involved.

It was somewhere during this time that we began to realize that an entirely new generation was arising that was markedly different from ours. Drug use among the so-called hippies, especially during the height of the Vietnam War, was unfortunately becoming an accepted way of life for many. Drug use among school-age children was still a relatively new problem.

We began to see the emergence of a mini-generation desiring to place its own mark on society's mores. Dress codes were drastically changing. Hairstyles were designed to astound the viewer rather than enhance the wearer. My generation's cherished way of life was being thrust aside as outmoded. It became our challenge to create an understanding among our children of the importance of their commitment to establish core values both in their personal lives and in the life of this nation.

In addition to the societal fallout as a result of the Vietnam conflict, no one was totally immune from being aware of the ongoing overriding social problems within our country. Within our transportation business, many of our trucker clients were based in the South.

Segregation was still an accepted fact of life. Many of the truck lines with whom we worked were domiciled in the South and Southeast. Many of them employed Afro-Americans drivers who lived in a strictly segregated society in their home states. However, when they were on the West Coast they escaped the stigma of second-class citizens and stayed in the same motels, ate at the same restaurants, drank from the same water fountains, and used the same restrooms as anyone else. In effect, they lived a double lifestyle.

For those of us living on the West Coast, it was an extremely uncomfortable situation knowing that on each round trip, descendants of slaves, constitutionally created equal by the Civil War, would have to return to a portion of our country where freedom's bell remained figuratively cracked. These were fine men (no women drivers then) who conducted themselves with unfailing dignity and courteousness. They, too, are an important part of the Greatest Generation.

It was during this time that a southern black Baptist preacher started to emerge from the pulpits of Georgia and Alabama. Dr. Martin Luther King, Jr. was soon to become a rallying force, along with Rosa Parks, for the elimination of racial discrimination in this land.

However, it is worth noting in recounting the societal contributions of the Greatest Generation that the repeal of laws allowing a two-tiered society in the south was undoubtedly made easier because of the opportunity presented to those of us who had served in the armed forces during World War II. We had learned to accept each other as we are. While limited segregation policies did exist within the military forces, men and women of all races and religious beliefs wore the same uniform and worked equally to defend the honor of this nation.

Twenty years had passed since the end of World War II. These were good years interspersed with the realization that the dreams of world peace and understanding that were among us at the war's end were still just dreams. World tensions, racial unrest here at home, and a deterioration of the family values within our society were still potent problems among us. There was a counterpoint to these stress points. Those of us who had served our country in time of great peril knew the importance of continuing our quest for a world of peace. Sooner or later the ultimate test of each of us became a determination to preserving our individual freedom through protecting our national security. Throughout the history of our ever shrinking world, no other generation had faced the grave international challenges that this nation faced and yet continued to prosper.

CHAPTER IV - BIRTHING A BUSINESS

OUR FAMILY RELOCATES

The summer of 1967 was a summer of change in our household. One of our customer friends informed me of a home for sale. It was located in the more upscale neighborhood of Sunnyside, located within a county island on the southeastern corner of metropolitan Fresno. After some negotiation with the seller, we arranged for its purchase by using another special loan fund, this time offered by the State of California to its World War II veterans. This opportunity was apart from the GI Bill Federal home loan provision that we used in purchasing our lovely starter home twelve years earlier.

So amidst some sadness coupled with the excitement of entering the next chapter in our lives, we left our memory-filled first home and our long time neighborhood friends and moved into a larger semi-rural residence. Not only would this change of location provide more creature comforts to our family but it would have an unexpected impact on our children. We remained in this home until the fall of 2005. At that time we downsized into a lovely home in a gated community in the neighboring city of Clovis.

Larry had just completed middle school and was enrolled to enter the recently opened McLane High School. This high school's student body was comprised primarily of Caucasian children of middle-income parents living in modest but well maintained starter home residences.

Upon moving to our newly purchased home in a long established more affluent neighborhood, Larry had to reenroll in Roosevelt High School in southeast Fresno. This was an old high school with a multi-cultural student body. While our home was situated in a semi-upscale neighborhood, the area comprising the student body for the high school consisted of students from all societal levels. It contained a strong contingent of Mexican-American and Afro-American students with a sprinkling of Asian-Americans. It was a new experience for Larry. He would later tell me that having an opportunity to interact with students of differing backgrounds was a great benefit in preparing him for adult life.

The same experience, naturally, held true for our daughter Gale. She had just completed elementary school and transferred into Kings Canyon Middle School. She, too, adjusted well to the multi-cultural student body.

I am proud to relate that both of our children were fine students who later attended and obtained degrees from California State University, Fresno.

As mentioned earlier, life in the '60s and early '70s saw the beginning of a growing drug culture in our community. For those of us who had children in school, it was a challenging time. We talked with our children about the problem and were quite surprised to learn how informed they were.

I once asked Larry how many kids he personally knew in his high school who used drugs. He counted on his fingers and finally told me "about twenty-five". When I asked him why he did not inform the school authorities about them, his response was that he and his friends were talking directly to the users about their problem. I interpreted this to mean that there was an unwritten honor code among the students. They seemingly would not "rat" on one another. Instead they would try to use their own peer pressure to alter the life styles of those who had become addicted.

While I cannot remember having such a specific discussion with our daughter Gale, she and her mother were very close and undoubtedly had a similar chat. We are both proud and fortunate to say that not once during their school years did either of our children do anything to bring discredit upon themselves or our family.

BACK AT THE OFFICE

At work my responsibilities continued to increase. In 1960 I was assigned the position of general manager. The company was progressing quite well. Its volume of business had increased substantially. The company was growing in personnel. I was overseeing a staff of over a dozen men and women. As our business continued to grow, it did so primarily because of the trust factor placed in us by our customers. Not only did we have reputable firms as clients, but officers and employees of those customers became close personal friends as the years went by.

The company was becoming nationally recognized because of our service level. We had set our standards and we were maintaining them. We had regional offices in Oregon, Arizona and New York. Althea and I enjoyed the opportunity to travel together to visit customers and attend conventions throughout the country. It was an exciting time of working with those businesses who subscribed to the same values that we set as standards for ourselves.

Then an unforeseen shadow arose. The founder of the company had reached his mid-seventies and decided he would reassume active operational control. Soon he was making commitments beyond our ability to fulfill them without lowering the service level that our customers had come to expect from us. It was a betrayal of faith to those who relied upon the performance levels that we had worked so diligently to establish and maintain.

Despite numerous conversations with the owner, he persisted on his course. I vividly recall questioning him about a specific action one day and his response was: "Don't question me. It worked in the '30s so I know it will work now." I respectfully tried to point out to him that it was no longer the '30s but the '60s and that business conditions were not the same. He was not deterred. Rightly or wrongly, I did not share these increasing stresses with my wife Althea. She was our homemaker. Our children were our gifts from God. Our home was our haven and my refuge. Providing for our family was my responsibility. I preferred not to bring home workplace stress.

By midsummer of 1971 I had decided that I could no longer be part of this betrayal. Our service level was deteriorating. Our company morale was in the basement. Working was no longer a happy experience. While I had an impressive title and had, for a number of years, top responsibility for the operation of the company, my income level was not what it should have been. We had a modest savings and a nice home but I did not have sufficient assets to start up a similar operation myself, or so I thought. I deemed it time to share my concerns with Althea. We had a heart to heart conversation. She said she would fully support whatever action I decided to take.

Therefore, on Thursday, July 29, 1971, I informed my employer that I was resigning and gave him a two-week notice of my departure. His response was that inasmuch as I was resigning, I should just clean out my desk and leave right then.

With two children of college age and with only minimal funding, with confidence that the road to success demanded doing things the right way, with almost twenty years of experience, and with strong moral support among those whom I respected in their chosen professions, I had jumped off of the diving board. Now it was time to swim.

"JOHANSON TRANSPORTATION SERVICE" IS LAUNCHED

I had decided that the transportation brokerage business was what I knew best. Despite my limited financial situation, I would see if I could create my own operation. No one outside of my wife knew of this impending action on my part until the day I resigned. I believed it would be improper to discuss the issue with current shipper and carrier accounts or my fellow employees while still on the payroll of California Trucking Exchange.

In retrospect, as self-serving as it may sound, it all came down to maintaining the high standards of personal conduct, which I espoused to others. I did not know what tomorrow would bring. I only knew that I had brought to an end my current untenable workplace environment. Interestingly, as I was bidding goodbye to my associates, four of them asked if they could work for me wherever I went. The assistant bookkeeper even said she would work for nothing because if I was leaving she was leaving also.

I spent the following week arranging to rent cramped office space at a local truck stop. I arranged to rent some desks and chairs. I arranged for telephone service. I opened an account with Western Union so that we could wire funds to drivers as needed. I opened a commercial checking account at a local bank. The same outside accounting firm used by my former employer agreed to help me organize an accounting system. The lawyer representing the legal firm that my former employer had used for many years could not serve as my counselor for ethical reasons. However, he placed me in touch with an excellent small law firm. A printing firm quickly designed a letterhead and check style. Three former associates left my former place of employment and joined me in this new adventure.

I also took time to visit a number of my former shipper customers. I informed them of my decision to open Johanson Transportation Service on Monday morning, August 9. To my astonishment, each of them stated without hesitation that they supported what I was doing. I received the same level of support from many of the motor carriers with whom I had established strong relationships. Success in this business is attained by maintaining a working balance between the amount of freight available to haul and the number of truckers available to haul it. It was an exciting week of preparation.

As promised, on Monday morning, August 9, 1971, for the very first time we answered the telephone with "Good morning, Johanson Transportation Service." Before the day was out, our work sheets listed dozens of shipments destined throughout the country. Carriers were available to transport them. We were off and running.

We were not, however, problem-free. Transportation brokerage is a very cash intensive business. Shippers are invoiced for freight charges immediately after shipment. Carriers expect to be paid immediately after delivery; which in most instances, is before the shipper has paid the freight invoice. Drivers needed to be advanced money to cover their operating expenses while en route to destination. Because we were a new company without a track record, the Western Union Company placed a maximum on the amount of funds they would wire for us in a single day. The agreement specified that they would be reimbursed fully the following day. We never failed to keep that commitment. However, few startup companies begin business with the volume of ours. Our need for Western Union's money wiring services, not obtainable elsewhere at that time, was critical to maintaining good relationships with our carriers and their drivers. In a nutshell, our promptness of next day reimbursement did not prevent Western Union from stopping us from wiring further funds once the daily maximum was reached. This action created operational difficulties for our young business that I felt were undeserved. It was a self-satisfying day when this type of money transmission was no longer necessary and we could dispense with their services.

I read once "few people are successful unless a lot of others want them to be." I remain humbled by the support of those shippers and carriers with whom I had worked for so long in my former environment. Almost all of them were determined to help our newly hatched company become successful.

For example, to help our limited funds situation, one shipper even sent us a sizable check with the notation "Advance on Freight." We hadn't yet sent him a freight invoice but he wanted to help our cash situation!

Another, whose custom was to batch freight bills at the end of the month and remit with one check, instructed his accounting department to pay each freight bill separately and immediately upon receipt from us.

It was gestures like these from a group of outstanding business friends that enabled us to realize that we had firmly grasped the bottom rung on the business world ladder.

Perhaps my greatest personal satisfaction during the ensuing months was to be able to return to an atmosphere of honesty, directness, and trust. The old saying, "a promise made is a promise kept," became our foundation. Our motto, "Experience--Integrity--Gratitude" remains intact as this is written thirty-five years later. Our small staff worked hard but in an atmosphere of harmony. Within a few weeks our volume had grown to include most of the accounts that we formerly served. Our son Larry worked as time permitted, while he pursued his post-high school education at Reedley College and California State University, Fresno.

It was not long before we learned that serious layoffs were taking place at our former employer's firm. We were informed that there was a pall covering the remaining staff members as the owner watched his business literally disintegrate before him.

In the spring of 1971 my brother Howard had moved with his young family to Portland, Oregon, to open an office for the California Trucking Exchange. With the imminent collapse of that company, in only a few months he resigned as well. He became a partner in our new firm in early 1972. While Howard is now retired, that office remains in existence today and is a strong component of our present multi-state structure.

It was not with a sense of revenge, but rather with the satisfaction of knowing we had validated the importance of setting high standards and doing one's best to adhere to them. Little did I know that only a couple of years later this policy would be put to its supreme test in our own organization.

By mid-fall it was apparent that the business would prosper. I often wondered how I could thank all of those folks who supported us through our startup months. Thanksgiving Day was approaching. I decided that we would have a Thanksgiving event. It would consist of an after-work reception at a local rural restaurant on the preceding Tuesday. We scheduled it between 5:30 and 8 p.m. It was basically an invitation to stop by on the way home from work. Our skimpy finances precluded anything other than salami, cheese and crackers and beverages of choice. What a joy it was to greet long-time business friends and modestly thank them for all that they had given to us.

While it has changed location, grown in numbers, and improved in quality, our company still expresses its thanks on the same day and during the same hours. It is always a pleasure for our staff to greet the retired, the newcomers and all of those in between. Long-time attendees are often heard to remark that our little party is the kickoff for the upcoming holiday season. Is there a greater happiness than the joy of being genuinely thankful?

TALK THE TALK OR WALK THE WALK

Prior to 1980 all interstate freight shipments were controlled by the Interstate Commerce Commission based in Washington, D. C. No interstate motor carrier could transport freight without having rate and route authority from this commission. They also controlled the freight rates charged by the railroads. The only exception to this rigid control was the movement via truck of unprocessed agricultural commodities. It was in this arena that our business functioned.

Our primary sources of tonnage were raisins, prunes, figs, dehydrated onion and garlic, dried beans and nuts. In addition all fresh fruits and vegetables were commodities available to us as freight sources exempt from I.C.C. regulation. Once a product had been processed to the extent that its identity was altered, it was considered a regulated commodity and subject to rate and route control. Regardless of commodity it should be noted that the I.C.C. had control over public safety for all land modes of interstate transportation.

While our newly formed company had an extensive customer base, almost half of our business at our Fresno office originated from a single shipper. It was regarding this high revenue account that I had to make a decision that would have a lasting effect upon our company. The Interstate Commerce Act was very clear in its description of regulated and non-regulated commodities. Natural raisins were an unprocessed non-regulated commodity for which we could legally provide carriers. Grinding raisins into a paste removed them from that category. By misrepresenting the grinding process, our major shipper was able to get an informal letter from a staff member of the I.C.C. stating that raisin paste was exempt for rate and route regulation by that agency. It was the shipper's intention to attach a copy of this non-binding unofficial letter to each shipment of ground raisins for which we were scheduled to provide truck transportation. By doing so it was assumed the trucker would avoid encountering problems with various state and national officials while transporting unauthorized cargo in interstate commerce. This was a flagrant attempt at circumvention of the law by my largest customer.

I had two options. My first option was to go along with the shipper and use the unofficial opinion letter as a basis for providing for trucking of the product. My second option was to stand upon the principles upon which my little business was founded. I decided to do the latter at the risk of losing my largest account. Without hesitation I wrote a letter to the Interstate Commerce Commission. In it I asked verification as to the authenticity of the letter in question. I pointed out the specific sections of the Interstate Commerce Act which it contradicted.

The response came not to me but to the shipper. It came quickly. The shipper was told that the staff member who wrote the letter did not represent the official position of the I.C.C. The letter further stated that the product in question did not fall within the "exempt commodity" classification. The commodity could only be transported by carriers having I.C.C. rate and route authority. The traffic manager of the shipper in question who had deviously procured the initial unofficial letter went to his president and informed him of my action.

I learned later that the president immediately called an administrative meeting. He was reported to have become livid with a table-pounding rage. Rather than censuring his department head for attempting to circumvent federal law, he issued a strict instruction that under no circumstances was their company to do any further business with our company. In one short moment we lost almost half of our volume. Standing up for one's principles and obeying the law of the land can be an extremely expensive combination. We had accepted the litmus test on our own integrity. Now it was time to pass it with a hard hit on our revenue.

As our company's history has unfolded, that action taken so many years ago proved to be not only morally correct but operationally wise. Without that customer's strong contribution to our revenue stream we were forced to seek out new customers. We were compelled to find new traffic lanes. We were inspired to move forward knowing that we had "walked the walk." And walk we did. Would we be where we are today if we had not pressed this difficult issue? I doubt it. Would we be a weaker company without this dramatic action? I think so.

To this very day I shall have the inner satisfaction of knowing that I followed my instincts and did what my inner voice told me to do. Is that part of our generation's legacy? As I write this, the officers and employees involved in that evasive scheme, including the president, have long since been dismissed. I am pleased to say we are once again serving this shipper.

Because our strength as a new company was based upon arranging for the transportation of dry freight, we had not made a serious effort to enter into the hauling of fresh fruits and vegetables. Our son Larry, upon joining the company immediately after his graduation from California State University, Fresno's excellent

Craig School of Business, was given the task of establishing our company in the business of transporting perishable commodities. He invited three of his fraternity brothers to join him and together they set out to establish a new dimension to our service area. A measure of their success is that today almost half of the shipments from our West Coast offices require temperature-controlled trailers.

As the years passed by, it became apparent that we needed an office on the East Coast to coordinate the shippers, receivers, and carriers who were located there. Shortly, we opened an office in New Jersey. During the years of the company's existence we have operated offices in Arizona, Washington, Nebraska, and Texas. As of this writing we have regional offices in Denville, New Jersey; Jacksonville, Florida; Madison, Wisconsin; Portland and Salem, Oregon, as well as representatives in several additional cities. We have recently established an international freight operation that will enable our company to offer our services to shippers, receivers, and carriers throughout the world. All Johanson Transportation employees are expected to "Walk the Walk."

THE COMPANY GROWS IN SIZE AND STATURE

As our company grew, so did our opportunity to join and participate in numerous trade associations.

Because a substantial portion of our business involved the transportation of dehydrated onion, garlic, and chili powder, we were invited to become members of the American Spice Trade Association. In the ensuing years I was asked to serve in such capacities as Chair of the Associates (Supplier) Group, general chair of a national convention, and Chair of the Western States Group, the only time such honors had been bestowed upon a non-spice dealer member up to that time.

As our company began developing the perishable shipping phase of our business, we were invited to join the United Fresh Fruit and Vegetable Association. A few years later I had the privilege of serving on the board of directors of that six thousand member organization. In addition I served as a member and chair of their Distribution Council during the mid and late 1980s.

The California Grape and Tree Fruit League invited us to become a member of their organization. We were the first transportation brokerage firm to receive such an invitation.

It was while serving as a member of these trade associations that I developed a keen awareness of the difference between membership in a trade association and membership within a non-profit association. Joining a trade association, including the local Chamber of Commerce, is a most effective way of promoting one's own business among peers and current or potential customers. Serving effectively on a trade association committee or board of directors can demand a significant time and resource commitment. At the same time it is also recognition of individual and corporate stature within that organization and therefore, primarily self-serving.

Admittedly the same rationale may be applied to service within non-profit public service oriented organizations. Everyone should devote a portion of his or her resources to public service. However, the underlying motive for joining and actively participating in non-profit public enhancement organizations should be the selfless opportunity to assist others less fortunate than us without consideration of personal or business return. More on this in the next chapter.

As our business prospered, so did our need for more office space. Only a year after launching our operation at Fresno's major truck stop in two adjoining 10′ by 10′ rooms, we expanded into a vacated barbershop on the same premises. We combined that space with a connecting larger office we built at our own expense.

Three years later we purchased some adjoining property and built our own small office building. In 1984 we doubled its size.

In 2005 our company took a major step forward when we relocated our corporate headquarters in Fresno to our own newly constructed 14,000 square foot professional office building. It is designed to accommodate our present and projected future needs for many years to come.

In 1971 businesses like ours preferred to locate at or near major truck stops to be accessible to truckers to hand them their loading instructions and cash operating advances. Today, with the development of modern technology in document and money transferal, this former need to be in physical contact with our carriers no longer exists. Presently all of our offices are located within professional office buildings.

From a founding staff of four, our company now comprises a corporate staff of approximately sixty employees headed by President and Chief Executive Officer Larry Johanson. He has carefully crafted an outstanding staff of highly skilled individuals committed to the standards established at our inception in 1971.

It is worth noting that staff turnover among our employees who have been with us two years or more is almost non-existent. Character does count and we are very proud that these traits are valued, protected, and exhibited among all of our employees.

As a separate division, we also conduct a vineyard farming operation headed by our son-in-law Jason Gomes. The operation consists of growing and drying Thompson Seedless grapes into raisins which are delivered to one of the packing companies that made up our original customer clientele list over thirty-five years ago.

CHAPTER V - SHARING VALUES

COMMUNITY SERVICE AS A WAY OF LIFE

As our company matured in staffing and our financial strength grew more secure, it was time to consider requests from additional non-profit organizations to participate more directly in their affairs through membership or direct donations of funds. It was not long before I began to receive requests to serve on various committees, boards of directors or boards of trustees.

It has always been my belief that no one walks alone through this life. Aside from one's faith values, there are those whom we hold in high esteem for their personal conduct. There are those whom we admire for their materialistic successes. Most of all there are those to whom we look up to for their compassion for those about them and their willingness to give of their time, treasure, and talent in volunteer service. As the years have unfolded, I have had a number of such people in my life. Central California community leaders such as Leon S. Peters, Lewis Eaton, Robert "Bob" Duncan, James and Coke Hallowell and others set examples of combining business success with community service for all to admire.

While I recognize that everyone's financial resources may vary widely, we are all granted the same number of hours each day in which to conduct our lives. From this platform comes the logical conclusion that I have strived to follow both professionally and personally:

"While no one can do everything, everyone can do something."

It is interesting to reflect on the origin of such a thought. Was it due to being raised in the Great Depression and having hungry and lonely men and women knock on our back door and ask for something to eat? Was it because of seeing starvation up close during my months in northern China? Was it because of seeing community heroes like those just mentioned giving so generously of themselves and their resources to try to make life just a bit easier for someone else?

In recent years the CEO of the Fresno Business Council Deborah Nankivell has been an inspiration to me as a baby boomer who cares deeply about the world around us. I admire her ability to combine her professional skills with her compassion to envision programs and ethos that will help bring about a meaningful and measurable transformation among us.

For whatever reasons, the desire to help others became more and more a significant part of my life. My parents and the parents of my wife Althea set examples of personal conduct that I both envied and aspired to replicate. Our children Larry and Gale have created within me a commitment to be worthy of their love and respect.

The '80s and early '90s were a time of great community activity aside from the responsibility of heading a growing business. As our staff matured and Larry assumed more and more of the administrative duties of the company, I was able to free myself from the constrictions of some of the demands of the day-to-day operation of our enterprise.

One of the first organizations we joined as a new company was the Fresno City and County Chamber of Commerce. In the mid '80s I was asked to serve on their board of directors. In the late fall of 1990 the president-elect was suddenly transferred to Seattle. I was asked if I would serve as Chamber president for 1991, which I agreed to do. The Monday morning following our installation dinner in mid-January three key vice-presidents resigned. They told me that they purposely held off their resignation announcements until after the formal inauguration because they did not want to put a damper on the festivities. It was only then that I realized that I had walked into a veritable hornet's nest of stifled communication and staff dissention. Unknowingly, I had embarked on a demanding year that would require major organizational restructuring including the dismissal of the executive director. With the cooperation of a strong board of directors and a dedicated executive committee, by year's end we had hired a new executive director and the Chamber was on its way back to effectiveness as the community's major advocate for business growth.

I was invited to join Rotary International in 1965 six years before founding Johanson Transportation Service. Rotary has had a significant impact on my life. Rotary's far-reaching efforts on behalf of world peace and understanding, coupled with direct participation in local societal improvement efforts are unparalleled among service organizations. In 1985/1986 I had the honor of serving as president of the Rotary Club of Fresno. In 1989/1990 I had the further honor of serving as the district governor overseeing forty-six Rotary clubs located throughout Fresno, Kings, Tulare, and Monterey counties.

The State Center Community College District granted me the privilege of serving as a member of their Foundation Board of Trustees from 1992 until 2000. I was left breathless when I was informed that Reedley College would present me with its Outstanding Alumnus Award during its graduation exercise in May, 1997. I was further honored in 2000 when the Community College League of California presented me with its Distinguished Alumnus Award, one of only six awarded throughout the entire state of California.

In 1998 Armstrong University, from which I had obtained my Bachelor of Business Administration Degree in 1948, honored me with a Distinguished Alumnus of the Decade Award for the years 1940-1950 as part of their eightieth year anniversary celebration.

Beginning in 1993 I was asked by the Fresno Unified School District to chair or co-chair four different school bond campaigns, the last two of which were resoundingly successful. I also served as a board member of their Public Education Fund for six years.

In 1997 I was asked by the Fresno Unified School District to serve as their community representative on the Joint Powers Authority Board set up to administer the affairs of the embryonic Center For Advanced Research and Technology. CART, as it came to be called, was a joint creation between the Fresno Unified School District and the Clovis Unified School District. The JPA Board consisted of the superintendent and a board member from each school district, a community member appointed by each district and a seventh member appointed by the Fresno Business Council. At the organizational meeting of that new board, I was asked to serve as chair, a position I held from 1997 to 2001. The academic program is built around a laboratory-based learning environment consisting of ten disciplines designed for high school juniors and seniors. Students spend a half-day at CART and the other half at their home high school. A total of eleven high schools are represented among the student body. With a capacity of approximately 1,400 students, the school is composed almost equally of representatives of the two school districts. It has grown to become a nationally recognized model for progressive educational techniques. At the conclusion of 2006, and as a current resident of the city of Clovis, I was asked by the Clovis Unified School District Board of Trustees to return to the CART Board as their community representative effective at the board meeting in January 2007. I was deeply honored to accept their request.

In 2001 I was persuaded to campaign for a seat on the Fresno Unified School District board of trustees during a most difficult time in their history. Immediately upon being elected I was voted by the newly assembled board to serve as president. The primary tasks of the four newly elected board members were to work with the three carry-over members to return the district to fiscal stability, replace ineffective leadership, restore internal morale, and reestablish public confidence. While still a work in progress, much has been done and the future of the school district is now back on a solid footing. It is now led by a newly-hired superintendent overseeing a revised senior administrative structure. Throughout the system there exists a reinvigorated cadre of dedicated teachers and support staff. Unfortunately, I was able to serve only a year and a half before being compelled to resign due to the time demands incidental to my wife's health.

Community Hospitals of Central California invited me to serve on their foundation board of directors. I served in that capacity between 1987 and 1995. Upon my departure I was made a director emeritus. In 2003 and 2004 I served as a member of their Operational Affairs Committee which oversaw (under the umbrella of the board of directors) the financial and operational affairs of the entire system.

I sat as a member of The Fresno Philharmonic Association Board of Directors for two years beginning in 1987.

In 1991 I accepted an invitation to join the Fresno Metropolitan Museum Board of Trustees where I served until 1997, including holding the office of president from 1993 until 1995. This organization was also suffering from morale problems brought about by ineffective leadership. During the second year of my presidency we were forced to replace the executive director. In 1999 I was honored by being named an emeritus board member of that organization.

In 1993 the United Way invited me to become a member of their board of directors where I served until

1997. I was awarded their prestigious George Osborne Spirit of Leadership Award in 1996.

In 1998, I was asked to join the board of directors for the Marjorie Mason Center, a home for abused women, during the transfer of that organization from the auspices of the Girl Scouts of America to a stand alone non-profit facility. I served for two years in that capacity at the specific request of Jackie Ryles, the former city clerk of the City of Fresno, who was the consultant employed to oversee that transition.

In 1997 a new faith-based organization called the Fresno Leadership Foundation was created. It was designed to help rebuild depressed neighborhoods from the bottom up rather than from the top down. I served as vice-chair of the founding board and chair of the executive committee from 1997 through 1999. The Fresno Leadership Foundation, which later changed its name to One-by-One Leadership, is an organization designed to explore each depressed neighborhood's hidden assets, create a vision for its residents to work to improve themselves; and to serve as an administrative and financial resource to bringing about measurable change. Their vision has proved to be highly successful. Today that organization is one of our community's finest examples of interaction among collaborative groups devoted to helping those with economic and social challenges.

Fresno Pacific University invited me onto their board in 2001 as a representative of the local business community while they were in the process of conducting a nationwide search for a new president. With this mission accomplished in mid 2002, I respectfully resigned. This is a highly esteemed faith-based institution of higher learning. It was an honor to serve them if only for brief time.

California State University, Fresno asked me to join their Foundation Board of Governors in 1992 where I continue to serve as of this writing including serving as a member of that group's executive committee and development committee.

Within the Craig School of Business at CSUF I had the privilege of serving as member and later chair of the Business Advisory Council and the Business Associates. I am also a founding member of the Family Business Institute.

In 2005 California State University, Fresno at its spring commencement ceremony, presented me with an honorary degree of Doctor of Humane Letters. As I stood on the platform before family, special friends, students, faculty, and administrators, I could not but think of the long road that I had traveled. As I accepted this award, I could do so only on behalf of so many who have had such a positive influence on my life in so many ways.

In October 2006 the CSUF Alumni Association presented me with their Arthur Safstrom Service Award for community service. When I was informed of the decision of the committee, I reminded the person who informed me of their action that I was not an alumnus. The immediate response, of course, was that my honorary doctorate did indeed qualify me.

I have listed all of the foregoing solely to emphasize that I believe strongly that the giving of one's time, talent, and resources to help others is part of the makeup of many of us who knew varying degrees of personal hardships in our young lives. Many people have referred to this process as "walking the walk."

There are over seven hundred non-profits operating within Fresno County. As I began participating in these service-minded entities I came to recognize one all too dominant factor among a number of them. Too many existed within a fortified castle surrounded by a moat filled with snarling crocodiles and with their drawbridges up. Each was highly protective of its interest area. To maximize the success of each there was a compelling need for these drawbridges to be lowered and the moats drained. There existed an immediate need for the creation of an interactive environment among all of them. Well meaning organizations were devoting significant portions of their energies trying to alleviate various problem areas that all too often overlapped. In the intervening years we have witnessed a significant change in transparency and collaboration through the strong efforts of the Interagency Council, the Non-Profit Council, the Fresno Business Council and others.

THE FRESNO BUSINESS COUNCIL IS FOUNDED

One of the most challenging aspects of volunteer work and talents to volunteer organizations was the frustration of interacting with many of our publicly elected officials. While there were examples of good men and women doing good work, there were also flagrant examples of self-serving individuals abusing public offices. They were all too often without qualifying skills and elected to offices to serve as puppets for vested interests. Some appeared to be overtly disobeying their oaths of office. Such conduct was casting a pall over our entire region. Out of this frustration arose a new organization designed to create a stronger relationship between the leaders of the business world and the public arena, as well as creating higher expectations for those elected to serve us.

In the fall of 1993 I had the privilege of being one of eight local business leaders who came together to explore the creation of a business-based organization similar to those recently created in Cleveland, Ohio and Stockton, California. It would come to be known as the Fresno Business Council. Convened by local attorney

Robert Carter, the premise was to bring together a relatively small group of successful business leaders willing to interface their management expertise with elected officials and staff administrators of public agencies, for the betterment of the community.

While not specifically stated, we were talking about lowering the drawbridges, draining the moats, and removing the crocodiles. This original group believed that an effective organization could be created with the singular challenge of bringing about a desperately needed improvement in our local economic and societal environment. At that time my belief was that we already had a Chamber of Commerce and there was no need for another one. We had to create our own distinct vision as a separate entity and determine what would set us apart in our efforts to attain it. Cleveland and Stockton had shown us that it could be done.

It was not long before our core group had grown to its maximum membership of one hundred business and professional leaders as provided in our by-laws. All were united in envisioning an organization quietly and semi-anonymously going about the business of creating change. Working for Mr. Carter was a new arrival from Minnesota. Deborah Nankivell came west with her young daughter and husband after giving up the active practice of law to become regional director for Common Cause in the Minnesota/Dakota region. Mr. Carter assigned her the task of performing the staff work necessary to create the Fresno Business Council. After a mountain retreat designed to set its course, the newly formed Fresno Business Council hired Ms. Nankivell to become its executive director. At our first subsequent board meeting we unanimously voted to have her become our chief executive officer in keeping with the universal title of the appointed leader of an established business organization. She continues to serve in that capacity as this is written.

In recognition of her extraordinary administrative and visionary skills as the C.E.O. of the Fresno Business Council, Ms. Nankivell was awarded the Civic Entrepreneurship Award by the California Center for Regional Leadership at its annual convention in San Francisco in 2006.

The Fresno Business Council's mission was specifically defined to raise the level of the lake for everyone afloat and not merely help individual members build bigger boats. This, to me, was to become the defining difference between the role of the Fresno Business Council and the role of the Chamber of Commerce. The missions for both organizations were complementary and both organizations were essential for a healthy and prosperous community.

By the end of the Council's first year, I was asked to assume the position of president and chair of the board of directors. I held those positions concurrently for the ensuing five years at which time I was given the title of Chair Emeritus. To say that it was somewhat intimidating to convene a meeting of the board of directors consisting of Central California's outstanding business leaders would be an understatement. Never had such a group existed. Concentrating on the areas of jobs, public policy, crime prevention and education, committees were established with the specific purpose of interacting with other agencies in order to leverage the effectiveness of each. Because of its limited membership, the Business Council oftentimes accepted the responsibility of assuming the role of convener. Our mantra was collaboration. Our task was to encourage participation in a transparent and interactive manner versus refereeing disputes between groups competing with each other from within their own fortified castles.

As mentioned earlier, one of the reasons for the formation of the Fresno Business Council was the questionable composition of the ethical character of some public officials particularly within the city of Fresno. As the years passed, some of those who had served on the City Council went to prison or were severely reprimanded for their inappropriate conduct in office. A strong effort was made to recall the mayor of the city of Fresno for his misconduct. Had the petitioners for recall obtained less than three hundred additional valid signatures he would have had to survive a special election in order to continue in office. While the Fresno Business Council did not formally take a position in the recall effort, many of its members did. Three of us went before the television cameras as concerned individuals urging support of the recall effort. For each of us it was a new experience to become directly involved in the unfamiliar world of political affairs.

During the intervening years the success of the initial vision of the Fresno Business Council has been reflected in such well known and eminently successful endeavors as the Collaborative Regional Initiative, the Regional Jobs Initiative, Choosing Our Future (a plan to transform central California's largest school district), the Central Valley Business Incubator, and assorted other local and regional programs.

The primary reason for the effectiveness of the council was its relative individual member anonymity. As a result, a few original members who clearly supported the goals of the council but desired personal identification as part of the council, became uncomfortable with the council's more anonymous approach and decided to withdraw from the organization.

Fundamental to all of these programs is an acceptance of the importance of the enthusiastic collaboration of caring individuals and organization. I would like to believe that some of the ideology referred to so often in this writing has been reflected in the vision as well as the action of the Fresno Business Council.

To what extent does this focus on collaboration come from the influences of the men and women who served in the various branches of our armed forces during World War II, the Korean War, and the Vietnam conflict? The necessity of interdependence and the establishment of trust are the key factors to survival. How much of this compassion for others is directly attributable to the "Greatest Generation?" How much is the result of the day-to-day toil of those talented men and women who are following? These are questions for others to answer.

It is sufficient to conclude that this nation, despite its abundant material resources, is unique because of the willingness of its people residing in a free democratic society, of whatever economic status, of whatever national origin, of whatever faith or lack thereof, to voluntarily join together to help make this a better place.

ESTABLISHING STANDARDS

It is valuable here to redefine and clarify some of the tenets that I have tried to follow throughout my life. I do so with the realization that some of what I shall write may be construed as self-serving. However, it could also be considered self-serving if I merely presented to those who may read this journal only a recapitulation of events and awards in my life without trying to identify the reasons for them.

Why was I asked to serve in all of these public positions? Mine was not the biggest business around nor the most important. Ours was not a well-known family name. I certainly was not a seeker of recognition. While admittedly a borderline Adonis, I would modestly hesitate to call myself exceptionally handsome! My conclusion at this stage of my life is that values became the determining factor. Those standards indoctrinated within me by my parents, the expectations of abiding by ethical principles in the life of our business, and a willingness to return some of what I had received - all became a vital part of the process.

I would also submit that much of my life's pathway was not of my singular doing. Rather, it has been with the hand of God, in whatever manner one wishes to place that context, holding onto mine. That guidance, coupled with inspirational heroes and the support of my family, have merged together to bring me to this wonderful phase of my life.

With that philosophical scenario as a starting point, allow me to offer some thoughts on those principles which I have tried to follow as a member of the Greatest Generation.

1. Trust and Be Trusted

Let's start with the simple matter of trust. Before one can be trusted, one must trust. In the course of my life it would be impossible to recall the number of times that I had exhausted my thought processes trying to determine a personal or business course of action. When I became groggy from knocking my head against the wall, I would suddenly remember to stop being so bull-headed and closed-minded. It was then I would begin to listen for the wisdom of an inner voice whispering to me. When my mind eventually became quiet, it was then that the answers I was seeking were oftentimes revealed to me. I learned to place trust in these revelations. It is a simple truism that the more one trusts an inner wisdom, the more one is committed to be a dispenser of trust.

Volunteerism is predicated upon mutual trust. Those who give of their time and substance to various charitably-based programs do so with a trust that such programs are legitimate and will carry out their proclaimed missions. Likewise, those same entities must utilize a basis of trust in expecting their volunteers to serve without selfish motives. It is when either side of this equation breaks down, that confidence in the mission of the organization erodes and third party trust, a.k.a. the public's confidence in the organization, diminishes rapidly.

To those organizations which have honored me with this trust, I express my deep gratitude. To the extent that I have been able to repay their trust, I am thankful. Were there mistakes along the way? Of course there were. However, honestly made poor decisions on either side, while regretful, are not an antithesis or the necessary enemy of trust.

When the Fresno Business Council was organized in 1993 one of our first requirements, if we were to become successful in our mission, was to establish public trust in our motives. Were we just a bunch of business "big shots" trying to pull a fast end run around an unsuspecting public for selfish gain? Or were we what we claimed to be - a new organization dedicated to improving the interaction between the public, non-profit, and private sectors for the benefit of our entire society? In the end, it was a combination of the formal actions of the organization itself coupled with the integrity of its key players that erased the initial apprehension and enabled the Business Council to attain the public trust it enjoys today.

2. Have Some Heroes

On an individual basis, the stature of such early area leaders as Leon Peters and Lewis Eaton were not gained merely because they were the CEO's of highly successful businesses. Each of these fine gentlemen was respected as a community treasure because of his openness to volunteerism and philanthropy in the development of our local service and cultural institutions.

While Mr. Peters and his family contributed, and continue to contribute, to our community betterment in a variety of arenas, his great passion was our Fresno Community Hospital system.

Mr. Eaton was an inspirational community benefactor with a particular emphasis on becoming the driving force behind the creation of the Fresno Metropolitan Museum of Art, History and Science.

Mr. Robert Duncan, Mrs. Coke and Mr. James Hallowell, the Honorable Robert Oliver and Dr. John Welty are shining examples of contemporary travelers whose deeds of generosity and inspiration continue to inspire us today. These men and women are showing us the way. It is now the challenge of those who follow in their footsteps to encourage our community to catch the vision of what we can accomplish under strong volunteer leadership by inspiring individuals.

3. Acknowledge Your Frailties

Don't be afraid to admit your mistakes. One of my early bosses told me that if I did not make any mistakes he would know that I was not doing anything. He added, however, that he would not expect me to make the same mistake too many times! Life's most difficult experiences occur when hidden past mistakes are uncovered and become major issues that could have been minimized or avoided completely had they been addressed when they occurred.

Recognize that others may disappoint you and that you will disappoint others. Accept that higher than realistic expectations by either side are an unavoidable component of everyone's life story. Happiness comes when those about you adhere to the same standards you desire for yourself. It is not in attaining perfection in a relationship but in the commitment to seek perfection that the rewards of friendship are realized.

Adjust to reality. While we all strive to idealism as we envision it, we need to be prepared to adapt to collaborative attainments. Such is the basis of democracy. Such is the reality of life.

Accept that knowledge can be intimidating while understanding that communicating effectively requires a full exchange of understanding of differing ideas. There is a significant distinction between either side being perceived as egotistical and demanding rather than each being eager to make a valuable contribution to a dialogue.

Finally, accept that from time to time you will unintentionally hurt someone dear to you just as they will unintentionally hurt you. Close friendships are both enduring and fragile. Protect and value them dearly. Out of the love of family and friends comes the peaceful sense of fulfillment of any member of a generation.

4. Accept Some Challenges

We can view our ethnic diversity as a chasm keeping us apart or as a bridge for understanding differing cultures and building upon the strengths of each. We can look upon the gap between our wealthy and our poor as a vast barren wasteland or as a fertile field that needs to be cultivated and harvested. We can look upon the academic stresses within our educational institutions as an uncontrollable fact of life or as a challenge that can be overcome through a stronger interaction between those within and beyond the system.

In summary, we are all sailing across a wide sea on a one-time voyage. Our challenge is to choose our vessel. We can look upon ourselves as passengers adrift upon a powerless barge or we can look upon ourselves as members of the crew on an empowered ship traveling a prescribed course to a predetermined destination.

5. Set the Bar Carefully

As I participated in the affairs of the numerous non-profit organizations enumerated earlier, there was one common thread among them. Those that were successful had an effective marriage between volunteers and staff. A carefully selected, trained, and motivated board of directors or trustees interfaced with an outstanding chief executive officer who directed dedicated professional personnel. Ultimately down the road, success depends upon the organization's professional leaders and leadership.

It is worth noting that during my service as president or on the boards of various non-profit institutions we approved removing the executive director or general manager of five of them for substandard performance. The first action of each of their replacements was to reestablish internal pride in the organization through higher expectations. Staff morale returned. Work performance improved. Renewed public interest followed. A new aura of enthusiasm for the institution's mission was recognized and supported throughout its service area. Everyone likes to be associated with success. High professional standards are fundamental to lasting success.

6. Create a Sense of Urgency

One of the missing components in too many non-profits, in my humble opinion, is a sense of urgency. Good leadership must overcome this complacency. Tomorrow may be too late for some vital operations. In 1984 I attended the International Convention of Rotary International in Kansas City, Missouri. Rotary had just announced an ambitious program, in conjunction with the World Health Organization, to eliminate polio from the world by 2005, the 100th anniversary year of the founding of Rotary. The featured speaker at one of the general sessions was Dr. Jonas Salk, discoverer of the Salk vaccine.

Dr. Salk began his address by thanking the organization for its willingness to undertake such a humane undertaking. Then this ninety plus year old icon of medicine presented those in attendance with an eye-opening challenge. His query was a simple one. Why must this magnificent effort take twenty years to accomplish merely to have it end on our organization's centennial year? How many lives could be saved through accelerating the program to its maximum? I am proud that Rotary accepted his challenge. Well prior to the beginning of this century polio had been eradicated from the entire globe except for an extremely few cases in remote areas of emerging societies

7. Don't Just Care – Act!

Our nation is great because of those who care. I am reminded of another speaker's searing remarks at that same convention of Rotary International. In discussing the role of volunteer organizations in bringing about a better world, he made this statement:

"Who cares if we care? Everybody cares. Caring without action is nothing."

Non-profits as well as private businesses move forward when those involved get a fire in their belly to make a difference. Just mouthing nice sounding phrases cannot replace the force of commitment. Look about you and observe those who really care and are doing something about it. Get on board. The challenge of caring and creating change leads me to this piece of advice I read long ago and have treasured for many years:

"If not now, when? If not us, who? If not here, where?"

8. Adopt a Code of Conduct

Some years ago the Leadership Fresno class created a statement entitled *"Community Values of the Fresno Region."* This statement of ten principles has since been adopted by most of the major organizations in this region. The Fresno Business Council was one of the first to do so. These values are:

(1) Stewardship
(2) Boundary Crossing and Collaboration
(3) Commitment to Outcomes
(4) Art of the Possible Thinking
(5) Fact-based Decision Making
(6) Truth Telling
(7) Power Parity
(8) Commitment to Resolving Conflict
(9) Asset-Based Approach
(10) Disclosure of Conflicts of Interest.

With every decision having to pass this stringent litmus test, whether personal or as part of a formal group, one's code of conduct is strengthened. Whether it is called an "inner voice" or "moral values," each of us is judged by the standards to which we subscribe.

Rotary International has a "Four Way Test" as its definer.

(1) Is it the Truth?
(2) Is it Fair to all Concerned?
(3) Will it Build Goodwill and Better Friendships?
(4) Is it Beneficial to all Concerned?

I support the person who said, "You can fool some of the people some of the time, but you can't fool all of the people all of the time."

9. Have a Confidant

There is an oft-used expression that says "it's lonely at the top." The only effective safeguard is to have someone in whom you have absolute confidence with whom to share your innermost concerns. My wish is that everyone will find just such a person. Whether it is a family member, a business associate, or a close friend, the ability to talk freely about private concerns and fully respect the counsel received is a priceless asset. To have such a person (or persons) in your life is a priceless gift from God.

10. Find a Mentor

One of the pitfalls of journeying through life is getting so caught up in our affairs that we think we can walk alone. There is no time in our lives when each of us cannot benefit from sitting at the feet of a mentor. For example, in my first post-college job the traffic manager of Sun-Maid Raisin Growers was a career mentor in guiding me into the logistics field that set the course of my subsequent business life. Since that time a number of close friends and business associates have provided advice to me on a number of issues that have arisen in my life. Find a person or persons to help smooth the way when the road gets bumpy and put lights on all the way through the tunnel.

11. Never Stop Learning

During this narrative, there has been one understated but underlying theme. Every turn in the road created an opportunity for a new experience. I think one of life's greatest joys is discovering what one doesn't know and striving to find the answers. The great joy of arising every morning is the anticipation of learning something new that day.

All of us have been subjected to the condescending verbiage of those unfortunate overbearing folks who would have us believe that they possess a supreme wisdom and are not in need of further knowledge. Within any organization extreme care must be taken to identify and isolate those individuals. Many are stereotypes who espouse maintaining the status quo under the guise of progressive leadership. Dry sponges have nothing to dispense when squeezed.

12. Love Kids

In the past twenty years or so I have received my greatest satisfaction from participating in those activities pertaining to the academic and social development of children. From working on school bond elections, to serving on the Joint Powers Authority Board for the Center for Research and Technology, to the Fresno Unified School District Board of Trustees, to my association with the Community Colleges of Central California, Fresno Pacific University, and California State University, Fresno, there is nothing more fulfilling than knowing one's efforts may positively affect a young person's life.

I urge all who read this to find a way to participate in all possible activities on behalf of young people. Read to a child. Volunteer in youth organizations. Open your checkbook. By whatever method is available, each of us needs to accept our individual responsibility in insuring that all children have every possible opportunity to maximize their innate skills.

Long ago I realized that expecting our school systems to educate our children within our school grounds during limited instructional hours is beyond their capabilities. Education is a seven day a week process every day of the year from the moment a child arises until bedtime. All of us, beginning with parents, must accept this challenge. Performance indicators reflect the validity of this mandate. Education is the ultimate collaborative in the real life world of joint ventures.

13. Be Inspired - Be Inspiring

The words of others who have captured some of my inner thoughts have always been an inspiration. When you are inspired, you will inspire others. Over an extended span of years I have collected quotations from widely scattered sources. They range from deeply profound to simple humor. Perhaps within them the reader may find some of the fundamental motivators that may have contributed to the aspirations of our generation. It is my hope that each person who reads this partial collection on the following pages will be moved to begin his/her own collection.

THE ELATION OF INSPIRATION

- When your work speaks for itself, don't interrupt.
- Few people are successful unless a lot of other people want them to be.
- One of the most difficult things to give away is kindness—it is usually returned.
- Success is a journey—not a destination.
- You can't make an error if you never touch the ball.
- Don't be afraid to take a big step. You can't cross a chasm in two small jumps.
- A nation's greatness resides not in her material resources but in her will, faith, intelligence, and moral forces.
- The shell must break before the bird can fly.
- The pleasantest things in the world are pleasant thoughts and the great art in life is to have as many of them as possible.
- Cast your bread upon the waters and it will return as buttered toast. (Joe Dale)
- Example is not the main thing in influencing others. It is the only thing.
- The more you listen to the voice within you, the better you will hear what is sounding outside.

- Care not so much what you are to others, but respect what you are to yourself.

- There is no definition of a successful life unless it includes serving others.

- You must be moving to stumble.

- God can't steer a parked car.

- If a man speaks in the forest, and there's no woman around to hear him, is he still wrong?

- Don't pour the concrete until you see where the people are walking. (Deborah Nankivell)

- Relationships, not programs, change lives

- God grant me the serenity to accept the things I cannot change, the courage to change the things I can, and the wisdom to know the difference.

- Nearly all men can stand adversity, but if you want to test a man's character, give him power.

- Character doesn't come from circumstances. It comes from choices . . .

- Friends are quiet angels who lift us to our feet when our wings have trouble remembering how to fly.

- I know in my heart that man is good. That what is right will always eventually triumph. And there is purpose and worth to each and every life. (President Reagan's Memorial).

- A true friend is someone who reaches for your hand and touches your heart.
- How old would you be if you did not know how old you are?
- Those who row the boat don't have time to rock it.
- Ethics is obedience to the unenforceable.
- A babbling brook cannot babble without rocks.
- By appreciation we make excellence in others our own property.
- If the only tool you have is a hammer, you tend to see every problem as a nail.
- Grandchildren are God's way of compensating us for growing older.
- A real music lover is a wife who applauds when her husband comes home at dawn singing.
- Happiness is not a goal – it is a by-product.
- A bone to a dog is not charity. Charity is the bone shared with the dog when you are just as hungry.
- Shall we call ourselves benevolent when the gifts we bestow do not cause us a single privation?
- The road to success is always under construction.
- Table manners change based upon the amount of food upon the table.
- Pain is inevitable. Misery is optional.

- The extra mile has no traffic jams.
- A voyage of discovery is not seeking new landscapes but finding new eyes.
- A truly happy person is someone who can enjoy the scenery on a detour.
- Be the change you want to see in the world – (Mahatma Gandhi)
- Those who stand tall do so because they are standing on the shoulders of others – (Bud Gaston)
- Procrastinate now!
- Water what you want to grow.
- Faith is a bird that feels dawn breaking and sings while it is still dark. – (Scandinavian saying)
- The only thing more expensive than education is ignorance. - (Benjamin Franklin)
- People don't care how much you know until they know how much you care.
- Reality is a challenging place to be.
- Pack your own parachute.

CHAPTER VI - PASSING THE TORCH

CLOSING THOUGHTS

It is my ongoing prayer that those who read this life journey will have a better understanding regarding where the Greatest Generation came from and where we strived to go. To the extent that we have succeeded in making this a better world, we are thankful. To the extent that we leave work to be done but have in some way inspired the future, we are also thankful. Our lives have been full.

To sum up our journey:

- We have been part of the needy.

- We have worked to create a world which, while still filled with desperate pockets of starvation, illness, tension, and tyranny, is free from the dominance of a worldwide dictatorship that would have engulfed us had we failed our duty to this nation and to our allies so many years ago.

- We have entered into an emerging new world of space travel.

- We are witnessing the creation of a borderless world economy, a transient population, and an unimaginable, worldwide, instantaneous communications network.

- We have accepted the moral and ethical values given to us by those who came before us and have done our best to enhance them and pass them along to those who will follow us.

- We are a thankful generation. It is impossible to adequately thank all who have touched my life, showing kindnesses in so many ways. I believe that God places each of us in a special place to serve His purposes. I have chronicled a summary of the various organizations that I have been privileged to serve. The confidence placed in me by being asked participate in, and oftentimes lead, so many public trust organizations humbles me.

- We are still a generation filled with pride and thanksgiving. I am forever grateful for having had the opportunity to be associated with so many fine community-minded associates. I have provided a list of various awards that have been presented to me. In many ways they have simply underscored the values that were shared by so many in my generation. These awards listed traits that we deem important in anyone's life. It is a privilege to have traveled over many highways as well as numerous byways to reach this time and place. I am grateful for every moment.

- We have been richly blessed.

May your life be filled with the full appreciation and adoption of those community values that filled our generation with meaning and purpose. Above all, don't try to emulate anyone else's life. Each of us has our own path to walk. No two paths are alike. Seek out your destiny and say "hello" to your own future.

Sooner than you can imagine your day of Thanksgiving will arrive. Gather about you those whom you love dearly. May you also include those friends and acquaintances that have been at your side during your life's journey. Together you will celebrate the joy that comes from being among those who have walked the walk with you as you strive to build your own legacy.

And that brings us to the beginning of a new journey - the future. The ultimate question then becomes relatively easy. How do we challenge and inspire those who follow, to accept and enlarge upon the mantle of stewardship as a core element of one's life? No one can do everything but everyone can do something. Starting today, new generations have within their grasp an opportunity to literally transform our world. Gigantic programs designed at high levels must become an available tool to each individual participant. Each of us, in our own way, will leave a footprint in the sand of life. And . . . the Greatest Generation is still making vital footprints every day, footprints which have become the legacy of our generation – a passion for stewardship.

And now a challenge from the Greatest Generation: May your footprints become a legacy highlighted by individual successes, co-mingled with a montage of working with and for the betterment of good people everywhere.

Finally, it is our hope that walking with our generation, living our history, sensing our values, and discovering our passions will help you define your generation as a people who succeed in transforming even more and bigger dreams into world-wide reality.

AN OPEN LETTER TO FAMILY AND FRIENDS

To my wife, Althea, of fifty-seven years at this writing, I am so thankful that I sat next to you on the Reedley College graduation platform so long ago. As a faithful homemaker and loving mother to our two children, you have always exhibited never wavering love and understanding. During the many meetings, conferences, telephone calls and study periods, your patience with the intrusion upon our private time together was unparalleled.

To our children, Larry and Gale, I am so proud of the each of you. I realize that you did not have your Dad at home as much as you might have liked when you were growing up because he felt that his duty was also in helping others. I oftentimes let those activities intrude into our quality time at home as a family. I appreciate your understanding that my efforts were always to try to do the right thing as I saw the right thing. One of the hardest parts of being a parent is that most of us only get one chance at it. For your ongoing love, I am thankful beyond expression.

For our daughter-in-law, Patti, and our son-in-law, Jason, Althea and I are both so thankful for the joy you have brought into our lives and the lives of Larry and

Gale. May the ongoing journey in your own lives be filled with the joy of appreciating those gifts of love you have shared with us. You each hold a very special place in our hearts.

To our three granddaughters, Amanda, Yvonne and Jody, my hope is that you will remember your Granddad as one who loved you very much. May you one day understand the commitment that Grandma and I had in trying to create a happy life for each of you. You are making us very proud of each of you as we watch your transformation from young children to energetic teenagers to charming young ladies. May your lives be filled with love and success wherever your paths may lead you.

To our many relatives and friends who are an unnamed part of this narrative, I thank you for your inspiration and your friendship. A trail as long as this one contains many side trips into fields of fond memories of happy times. It would be impossible to review them all. I treasure each one.

To my counselor and confidant, Deb Nankivell I thank you for your encouragement in suggesting that I write this journal. I have deeply valued your wisdom in helping me cross rocky streams and rushing rivers. You have guided me in my efforts to help build the bridges necessary to transform a hurting community.

To Dr. John Boogaert and his wife Brooke for your invaluable help in bringing this book to life through your inspiration, insight, and editing skills.

To my contemporaries who underwent similar life experiences including the turmoil of World War II, I fervently believe that Mr. Brokaw is correct. With a sense of unfeigned pride I believe our generation comprises a group of men and women who probably understand as much as any other group of individuals in our nation's history how precious our freedom is and how easily it can be tainted or lost through trepidation or inattention. Democracy is all too often accepted as our birthright without thought as to our responsibility to protect it.

As the shadow of the Greatest Generation lengthens over the highway we have traveled together, may those who continue the journey take inspiration from what we tried to accomplish, forgive us for our shortcomings and realize our unfulfilled determination to enable this great land to one day attain its constitutionally defined destiny.

Lastly, such an all-encompassing acknowledgement would not be complete without thanking God for protecting and directing me through this fascinating journey. May we always recognize that our earthly and spiritual needs are inseparable.